The Best WINE in the SUPER MARKET

Written and illustrated
by
James Page-Roberts

W. Foulsham & Co. Ltd.
London · New York · Toronto · Cape Town · Sydney

W. Foulsham & Company Limited
Yeovil Road, Slough, Berkshire, SL1 4JH

ISBN 0-572-01389-2

Copyright © 1986 James Page-Roberts

Printed in Great Britain by
St Edmundsbury Press Limited, Bury St Edmunds, Suffolk

CONTENTS

LET'S KEEP IT SIMPLE

Before we even consider what supermarket wines to buy, or whether they would suit our taste and pocket, we should know a bit about the making of this delectable liquid. Then we can get on to the detective work of wine – that is, having a reasonable guess at what's on offer by simply looking at the outside of a bottle.

After that, we investigate the various wine-producing districts of the world and the outlets where they can be obtained.

To make wine-selection a little easier when you are confronted by those batteries of bottles in major supermarkets, I offer the names of some of the best quality, best value wines to place in your trolley or basket.

I have used the simple price guidelines outlined here.

Anything (£−2) needs our close attention. *That* is what we are after – good, cheap wine. And that is what this book is mainly about.

Then, (£2−2.50) and (£2.50−3) will give a fair price-indication of wines to try in the 'better' range.

Port, Champagne, good claret and Burgundy, etc. are clearly in the upper price bracket – where a pound or two, for those wanting to buy them, will not mean so much. But those I do mention, priced (£3+), will be of good value.

Violent budgets, greed, inflation and fluctuation of monetary exchange rates, of course, can bring about changes at any time. And after a swingeing budget, it is always difficult to know if a merchant will absorb some or all of the penalty, add it on in full or take advantage of it to raise the basic price of the wine as well. So it often takes quite a while after such an upheaval for prices to settle so that comparisons can be re-made.

Then there is the matter of sweetness and dryness in a wine. As our opinions often tend to differ from the sellers' descriptions on labels, take it that all white wines are dry to just-sweet and that reds are all on the dry side – unless otherwise noted.

Will the bottle be there on the shelf when you come to buy it? We cannot be sure when just writing about one in glowing terms could start a rush – and thus cause a shortage.

But supermarkets do handle enormous quantities of wine, and their buyers have the skill and foresight to maintain the quality of a successful marque.

One must remember, too, that smaller branches of a big chain of shops may only stock a limited range of wine.

In the main, the following opinions are mine, though, in a few instances, I have had to rely on those of the wine buyers.

So let us start on this simple approach to a subject that tends to become confused by long lists and shrouds of elitism. The enjoyment of wine need be no more or less than natural, no-nonsense FUN.

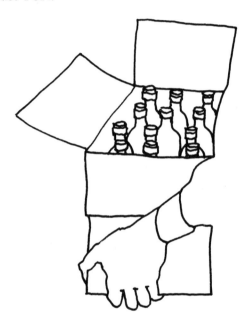

THE PRICE OF WINE

Expensive wine is not necessarily good wine, or wine that you will like. Cheap wine is, in fact, a surer bet since it is made to be 'popular'.

Costly wines only concern you when you want to celebrate (as with Champagne), to keep for a while to mature (to lay down), to impress someone (a potential spouse, perhaps, or the boss) or to relish when you have acquired enough knowledge and experience to fully appreciate it and so to justify the cost.

If you agree with that, we will look, in this guide, for what most of us are after – sound, modestly-priced wines from supermarkets and specialist wine stores. And in looking for these wines, there are many surprisingly good bargains.

It could be a supermarket 'loss leader'. It could be the end of a purchased lot which must be sold quickly to make room for a new line. It might not have been as popular a wine as anticipated, or it may have to make way for a quick-turnover wine to improve cash flow. It could have thrown a sediment of some kind (never a bad thing) and appear to be unacceptable on the strength of it. Or it might be that a merchant has bought a huge quantity and wants to make his profit over high volume, low mark-up sales. And I'm sure there are other reasons, too.

You must never be put off by these 'bargain' wines. Buy one and be prepared to return immediately to buy more if the wine and its price pleases you. That 'immediately' is important. Others will be thinking on the same lines and may get back before you do to snap up the rest.

At Christmas time, certain wines are reduced in price to catch the festive trade. That is a good time to stock up.

Really bad wines are seldom on offer. There is too much business and reputation to be lost by taking such a risk.

But from wherever you buy your wines, it pays to be friendly with the head of the wine department. Regularly ask their advice. Show interest and they will respond – to your joint pleasure and advantage.

WHAT IS WINE?

When sweet grape juice has, at vinification time, reacted with yeast on the skins (or added yeast) and turned sugar into alcohol, it has become wine. And, as a by-product, carbon dioxide gas is released.

Simple? Yes, but this basic process can be interpreted in so many ways that few people drinking the wine will have much idea of how that particular brew was handled.

I will only describe one method – the basic one.

I mentioned sugariness. Sometimes there is not enough of it in the grape juice to raise the final alcohol content to the required amount for pleasure or preservation. Sugar, or a sweetening agent, is then added to the grape juice (called must).

This extra sweetness can take the form of concentrated grape juice, or sometimes it is plain and simple sugar – the kind we use at home.

This addition is sometimes frowned upon or even banned. But in years when there has not been enough sunshine to create adequate sugar in the grapes, the practice of adding it is more widespread than imagined.

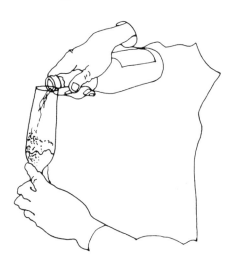

VINE TREATMENT

Before the grapes ever reach the winery, a year's hard work has gone into the vineyard.

Pruning, in northern climates, has been an arduous and cold, winter job.

Manuring may have taken place. The ground will have been cleared of noxious weeds. Earth may have been carted from lower terraces to higher. Green manure may have been grown and dug in. Straw may have been incorporated into the soil. The ground will have been tilled.

Owners of every vineyard – from a plot of a few vines to those of many hectares in size – will have their own ideas on how to conduct these annual tasks in order to make good wine.

But, with few exceptions, vines are prone to disease throughout their growing season. And prophylactic treatment is more effective than tackling the disease after it has started. So sprays are needed to keep the vines and their grapes healthy.

Therefore, depending on weather conditions and grape varieties, decisions must be made on what sprays to use, how often to apply them, how strong they should be and when to stop. This latter is a crucial decision to make, as to spray too late and in dry conditions (when rain will not have washed off surplus spray) will allow that spray to reach the vinification – and some of the chemicals used are pretty nasty.

Fortunately, there are moves afoot to reduce sprays and even eliminate them altogether. But these ideas on vine culture are in their infancy, and the products from them seldom reach our supermarket shelves.

HARVEST AND FIRST PROCESSES

Gathering grapes can be done by a happy and very hard-working labour force, or accomplished in a fraction of the time by mechanical harvesters.

For the finest wines, where selective judgement is essential, the former method holds sway – and will continue to do so. For bulk wines in huge vineyards, the latter is speedily taking over. Even in small 'quality' vineyards, picking machines are more and more to be seen at harvest time.

Squashing the grapes to extract their juice may be done by foot. This is a fun if slippery job that can be sweaty in hot climes and freezing in cold ones (like in England). It is seldom done nowadays but, surprisingly, is one of the most delicate ways of breaking the grape skins yet not bruising pips and stalks – which can add unwanted flavours to the wine. This jolly treading on the grapes at harvest time has almost entirely been taken over by machines that extract the stalks and break the skins.

At this stage a lot of what is called 'free-run' juice flows naturally from the skin-breaking process. This, in the case of white wine, is ducted away into wooden, glass, resin, concrete or stainless steel tanks to be fermented on its own or to be mixed with the juice squeezed from the remaining bulk.

The solid, dry residue may be returned to the vineyards as fertilizer or have water, sugar and yeasts added to ferment once more in its own right.

The resultant liquor from this extra fermentation is distilled into a spirit called Marc, Grappa or such. Its taste (over the alcoholic haze) is rather like that of crunched grape pips.

Wine may be distilled to become brandy.

Wine is also distilled to become plain alcohol. Wine 'lakes' can then take up less space.

FERMENTATION STARTS

The white grape juice that we have seen extracted from the fruit by crushing and squeezing, will now be run into fermentation vats – and may have sugar and yeast added. Acids, sulphur and other items may be included at this stage, too.

The natural or induced temperature in these fermentation vats will govern the speed at which alcohol is produced and carbon dioxide gas is given off. And this will have a strong bearing on the style of the finished product.

In the case of red wines, the pips and skins (and sometimes stalks) will all be included in this initial fermentation process – that is, until enough colour, tastes and tannins have been extracted from them. The liquor will then be strained and the residue squeezed.

In the case of correctly made rosé wines, when just a little colour is needed, this skin-inclusion will be a very quick one.

The coloured juice, to be turned into either red or rosé wine, will now be treated in the same way as white grape juice – with the yeasts continuing to turn sugar into alcohol.

Do we let the yeasts turn all the sugar into alcohol to make a dry wine, or stop them from completing their task to produce a sweet wine? Or do we ferment out to obtain the desired degree of alcohol and then add a sweetener of some kind?

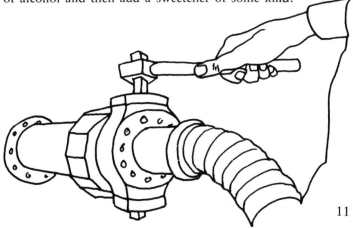

FERMENTING OUT FOR DRY WINE

The simplest method of fermenting grape juice into dry wine is to allow natural and/or added yeasts to tackle the sweetness and let nature take over to complete the job.

Depending on the temperature and what appears to be a double fermentation, this may take from a week or two to many months.

In English and north European conditions, for instance, the weather is cool at fermentation time. So reaction between yeasts and sugars will be slow. They may stop altogether in very cold weather and start up again when it gets warmer. The second (malolactic) fermentation may then take over.

In the meantime, and before the bottling, the wine may have been racked (run off from above the dead yeasts and such that will have fallen out of the solution) and filtered several times. Some purists neither rack nor filter, maintaining that each of these processes will extract certain qualities from the wine.

So, left to nature, it may not be until the spring following a September to November harvest that the wine will be ready to bottle.

There are exceptions, of course. Nouveau wines are rushed. While others will spend another year or more in vat or cask before being bottled.

STOPPING FERMENTATION FOR SWEET WINES

We have just considered the complete fermentation of grape juice into dry wine – when all the sugar was turned into alcohol by the yeasts. But just-sweet wine is popular, as is sweet and very sweet wine.

The processes of fermentation can be stopped before all the sugar has been converted into alcohol (thus leaving a sweet wine) by adding sulphur, subjecting the wine to heat, straining very finely to extract those hungry yeast cells, adding chemicals, centrifuging, adding alcohol and probably by other means. Or, sweet white wines may be obtained by fermenting out and adding purified (unfermented) sweet grape juice or sweeteners.

But should any live yeasts remain in this sweet wine, they will continue the fermentation in warm conditions – with the resultant bursting of bottles or blowing out of corks. So to rid this wine of yeasts is important.

An exception is when extremely sweet wine is concerned. In this case, the sugar content is just too much for the yeast cells to tackle. The conditions then are rather like you or me trying to swim in a pool of golden syrup.

Another exception is when yeasts are left in bottles of Champagne to create the wine's sparkle. But we will deal with that later.

COLD FERMENTATION

As fermentation temperatures are beginning to be held under stricter control, so vinification methods may improve.

Where we really notice this is in the cold fermentation of white wines from hotter climes and in the lower price bracket. And cold fermentation is becoming all the rage.

The equipment needed is extremely expensive – using stainless steel and refrigeration. But manufacturers feel that the high capital cost is justified as fewer mistakes will be made in the future and a more uniform product can be offered for sale. The chances of making a drinkable wine in a bad year are greater, too.

What is cold fermentation? The grape juice is fermented at a low temperature for a longer time than is usual. These conditions produce a clean, fresh, almost lemony wine.

This process is certainly now a winner for those perfecting the method. The wines sell extremely well. There are some snags, however. The wines are beginning to taste rather alike – from wherever they come.

Imagine a bottle of clear, cold, spring water. Add some lemon juice, some dissolved peardrop juice and a dollop of alcohol. That will give you a general idea of the taste. And very nice it is, too.

But if this movement toward the 'sameness' of cold fermentation wine continues, there could be a reaction against it – as there has been in the beer world with the campaign for real ale.

Should you come across a dull, white wine, it can be enlivened by sloshing in a little blackcurrant concentrate (Cassis for preference) or sloe gin (home-made if possible). In fact, any flavouring may be added. There are no rules.

WINE AND WOOD

There are wines made for drinking as soon as they are marketed (or destined for further hoarding after purchase by the consumer) that have been aged for a time in wooden barrels.

Time in these barrels speeds the maturing process and imparts welcome tastes to a wine. New barrels add flavour more quickly.

Oak is the timber most favoured. It is porous, and this allows for quicker ageing/oxidation to take place and more taste of the wood to be taken up by the wine. And the flavours of oak and wine do seem to marry extremely well.

Owners of the greatest Bordeaux châteaux and dedicated makers elsewhere, favour the use of fresh wooden barrels for all or most of their new wine. Winemakers in the bodegas of Rioja favour old, well-used casks in which to rest theirs.

Both red and white wines benefit from lying in oak. But to arrange it takes time, trouble and money. So wood-aged wine will always cost more than that made with less care, attention and investment.

CHAMPAGNE

In most peoples' minds, wine with a sparkle to it means sipping or swilling at a 'celebration' or 'special occasion'. And there is something about a wine with bubbles in it that transports even plonk ingredients into a drink of style.

At the top of the tree stands Champagne, king of all imitations because of the basic wine and of the intensity of its bubbles.

This is made by fermenting out white wine (often extracted from red grapes) and giving it another fermentation in its own, sealed-up bottle.

The sediment so created in the 'bottle fermentation' period is expelled by a neck-freezing and ejection process. The loss of

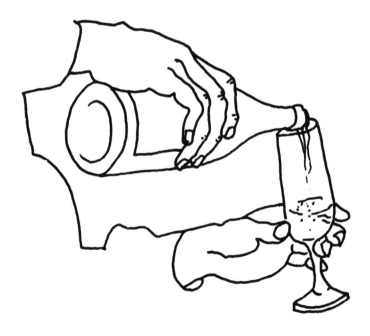

liquid volume so created is then made up by adding wine and sugar 'to taste'. A cork is inserted, and hey presto, Champagne.

Now, there is one important point to make about this fine and expensive beverage. The longer it remains in its bottle after it is made, the better it becomes – whether it is a 'vintage' (from a good year and made with special attention) or not. So, if you can possibly manage to buy well before that 'occasion' you will be doing the wine and yourself a good turn.

'Demi-sec' and 'sec' wines contain varying degrees of sweetness (not a bad thing in Champagne). 'Brut' means dry.

CHAMPAGNE SELECTION

Most wine vendors sell Champagne – all with a price tag, naturally, over £3. The brand leaders, in Moët & Chandon and Mumm, are both excellent. You need not pay their prices for a good example.

Marks and Spencer have a fine and popular brand.

Waitrose, too, have one of the best.

Arthur Rackham/Winefare have a good selection.

Majestic Wine Warehouses offer several varieties.

Peter Dominic choose well. Their Lambert is excellent.

Threshers sell thirteen kinds.

Sainsbury's own brand is a winner.

British Home Stores have a good Champagne.

Presto are justifiably proud of theirs – as are **Booths.**

Drew and **Cellar 5** consider their own Champagne, René Florancy, to be about the best value for money in their whole range.

SPARKLING WINES AND HOW TO TREAT THEM

Champagne should be cooled – but not too much. Otherwise you will miss the very classiness for which you are paying.

Drink it to celebrate, to surprise the cook in the kitchen, perhaps in the bath or on the most romantic occasions. Consume it with imagination. It is a great wine and a great restorative.

If Champagne stands supreme as the great sparkling wine of the world, there are a mass of others, made by the same method – and by other, less intensive ways – that are often almost as good.

Let's look at these other methods.

Some white wines are fermented in the bottle, as in Champagne, then tanked, sweetened and filtered back into bottles again.

Other wines complete this whole fermentation and re-fermentation process in tanks, and are then sweetened and filtered into bottles.

Some just have carbon dioxide forced into the wine, using the same method as in soda water or other sparkling soft drinks.

When buying these sparklers, you may be assisted in your detective work by noticing on the label: Champagne Method, Bottle Fermented, Tank Fermented (Cuve Close and Charmat are the same), or nothing (probably carbonated). Mousseux simply means fizzy. I often wonder if the 'method' makes all that much difference.

Anyway, the lesser the quality of the wine, the colder it should be for pleasurable drinking.

Good sparkling wines to seek out are Blanquette de Limoux, Sparkling Saumur or Spanish Cava. These are not copies of other wines. They are very much 'their own thing'.

For the sweeter-toothed, aim for those bottles that have 'sec', 'demi-sec' or 'rich' printed on the label – or go straight to Asti or Moscato Spumante.

If you want to elevate an ordinary sparkling wine to realms of class, turn it into Champagne cocktails – a fine wedding drink. Put a pinch of sugar into a glass, then a couple of drops of Angostura Bitters. Now add a measure of brandy (it can be a cheap one) 'to taste'. Then top up with very cold, dry fizz. It will tend to bubble over in the glass – and in your mind, too.

A wide selection of these sparkling wines is to be found on all high street wine shelves.

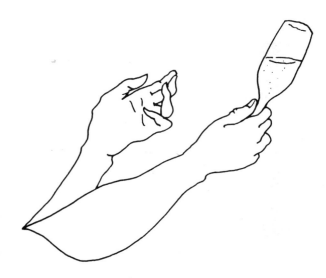

SPARKLING WINES SELECTION

Sekt is a sparkler from Germany. **Asda, British Home Stores** and **Fullers** have them (£2.50–3).

Carrefour sell the Spanish Cava wine Monistrol (£3+). And **Bottoms Up** offer the frosted-glass bottled Castellblanch (£3+). Spanish Cava (sparkling) wines such as these are to be found in many wine stores. With their high quality and reasonable price, they are well worth a try.

Waitrose offer the fine Blanquette de Limoux and a superb Crémant (creamy rather than fizzy) d'Alsace (Dopff) (both £3+).

Peter Dominic have a Crémant from the Loire and their reliable Le Piat Crystal (both £3+).

Threshers sell a great deal of Veuve du Vernay (£3+) – a sparkling wine that is generally available.

Oddbins, Gough Brothers and **Majestic Wine Warehouses** offer one of the best value sparkling wines in their Cavalier (£2.50–3).

Moscato Spumante is one of the most popular and widely sold of all sparkling wines. Its price (£2–2.50) is much in its favour. You can find it at **Carrefour, Augustus Barnett, Fine Fare, Presto, Davisons, Saverite** and **Walter Willson** among others.

And **Fine Fare** also have a splendid sparkling Saumur (£3+). **The Victoria Wine Company** sell it, too, as do **Threshers, Sainsbury's, Morris's Wine Stores, Gough Brothers** and more.

Cullens sell an excellent Neufchatel in sec and demi-sec form (£2.50–3).

Lay & Wheeler offer a fine Rôbe d'Or (£3+), as do **Townend** and **Tanners Wines** (three class merchants).

Le Riche's sell an Austrian Hock Riegal for (£2.50–3).

And Sparkling Blue Nun (£3+) goes well in **Agnew Stores**.

Hillards sell the British Tiffany (£2–2.50).

Morrisons offer Cabrera at (£2–2.50).

Lo-Cost's best seller is a cider (looking like Champagne) called String of Pearls (£–2). **Carrefour** sell it, too.

Airey's Wine Stores sell Baron de Beaupré (£3+).

Dickens Wine House offer Duc de Florincourt (£3+).

Dolamore sell Club Prestige (£2–2.50).

Grandways stock Framar Spumante (£2–2.50).

Blayney Wines recommend their sparkling André Gallois Blanc de Blanc (£2.50–3).

An unusual sparkling wine may be obtained from the **Russian Shop** (in High Holborn, London). It is Krim (£3+), and red in colour.

'LAYING DOWN' WINES

Having bought yourself several bottles, you will need to store them.

A proper wine rack will do for this. Or, cheaper still (or free) would be a plastic milk or soft drinks crate (on its side). Or, when all the wine is the same and you will not want to withdraw one bottle from beneath the others, box frames, made with 7 × 1 inch (17 × 2.5 cm) timber, halved at the joints, resting on the floor and mirror-plated to the wall will do the trick. Twenty-eight bottles will fill an area of 19 × 14 in (48 × 35 cm), though this space may be sub-divided to store smaller quantities by building-in batten rails on which to rest further shelves.

Claret bottles are happiest on top of each other, Burgundy bottles less so, and tall, Mosel-type bottles least so. These will tend to slip forward.

A cardboard wine box on its side is the least satisfactory. It will buckle, sag and bend.

Having bought a bottle or two for future drinking, you are, in fact, laying down wine. You now have a 'cellar', like it or not.

This store of wine should be in a dark place, out of sight, and where the temperature does not rise and fall at speed. And it should be under lock and key if there are those around whom you cannot trust!

Extreme heat and cold, if reached slowly, does not greatly affect wine – except that heat will mature it more quickly (and the corks might weep a little) and cold will precipitate sediment (and, in white wine, crystals).

Both these latter developments will indicate that the wine has not had all its guts filtered, frozen or centrifuged out of it at the winery. So the omens are good.

'CELLAR' WINE, AND WHAT TO LOOK FOR

What wines are candidates for your store?

White wines are usually best drunk young – except for some great and expensive ones. But a few are useful to have in your cellar – just to extract when wanted.

Reds, however, generally improve with time in the bottle – except those in litre bottles.

The key word here is tannin. Tannin comes in tea and appears in wine as a substance that puckers the mouth. This is not at all the same as sourness – which is probably caused by vinegar bacteria. Such wines as these do not often appear nowadays – with highly skilled technologists at the helm.

Tannins come from stalks, skins and pips. They preserve the wine. And as they become less pronounced over the years in bottle, the wine becomes softer, mellower and grander.

But in the general scheme of things, wines are marketed as being ready to drink right away.

However, there are plenty of new wines that *must* be laid down to be at all drinkable. And there are others that are fine to drink when bought but will still improve greatly if given time.

Wines made solely from certain grape varieties should be thought of as possibilities for your cellar.

Those magic words 'Cabernet Sauvignon' on the label usually mean that the red wine from this particular grape variety has possibilities as a keeping wine.

Another grape to look out for is the Syrah – or Shiraz to some people.

There are others, too. But these two varieties are grown all round the world and in every conceivable soil and climate. And as they are vinified in different ways, they can vary a great deal. That means in price as well as quality, so some will be bargains.

But when it comes to choosing 'laying down' wine from a particular district, it is to Bordeaux that one must look.

Called claret, this wine, made in a sunny, dry year, is the obvious first choice. But it can be expensive. If, however, there have been one or two good years in a row, then a bottle just stating Claret on the label will have come from one of these vintages. Its price will be much lower than château-bottled wine and will, therefore, be a good value candidate for your 'keeping collection'.

The Balkans (those countries between the Black Sea and the Adriatic, such as Hungary, Yugoslavia, Romania and Bulgaria) are producing better and cheaper wines all the time. Look there.

And the upper Rhône valley and south-west France are other prime areas for search.

Rioja, with the key word 'Crianza' on the back label, is yet another.

Côtes du Rhône is not often one to aim for. But should you see that a bottle of this wine is made partly, or wholly, from the Syrah grape – you're on.

LEARNING FROM YOUR STORE

If you can wait a month, or even a year, after putting those red wines in your 'cellar', so much the better. Make sure that they are lying down – to keep the corks moist and airtight. Then, if you replace bottles that you have extracted, and add some occasionally, you will be starting to build up a collection – albeit, perhaps of modest wines. But it is a start.

If you are keen to do this, buy a hard-backed ledger as your 'cellar book'. Record the wines and your description of them when introducing them to your collection. Mark down the date, source, price, cork length, quality and brand, colour of the wine, smell, taste and aftertaste. Then, when next you try a bottle (try to make it a year), and without looking at the previous comments, record the wine again ... and again.... This is a wonderful, self-instructive way to learn about your critical faculties – and the way your wine is maturing.

DECANTING

There are several reasons for decanting wine.
1. The boss may be coming and the wine is not as fine as you imagine he is used to.
2. The wine may have thrown a sediment. This will be perfectly acceptable in the bottle if it has been standing up for some while, when the gunge will have settled into the punt (the concave bit you see if you look at its bottom). The wine will be clear until you reach the last glass or two – when cloudiness will spoil its appearance.

(Incidentally, it is a good practice to pour wine gently. And if you always keep the label uppermost, there will be even less chance of any sediment becoming mixed with the wine.)
3. You may have a fine decanter that you want to show off.
4. You could taste or smell sulphur in the wine. And if this is the case, put your thumb over the top of the bottle and give the whole thing a good shake or two. Then decant with aplomb.
5. And then there's the very good reason of letting red wine 'breathe'. Of course it doesn't breathe, it takes up oxygen and 'ages'. Test this for yourself with full, rich, red wines to see what happens over several days. But loosely stopper them to keep flies and noxious bacteria from spoiling the wine.

Any white wines that have been decanted should be drunk up sooner than red. Some whites do improve – but not many. Red wines usually get better.

And here's a note on glasses. Shapes don't really matter, but to store your glasses upside-down will enhance the smell of the shelf – not the wine.

BOTTLE VOLUMES

The volume of wine offered for sale (nearly always printed on the label or, if not, moulded into the glass at its base) is important.

Sadly, most 'everyday' bottles in the U.K. contain 70 cl. There are occasions when this 'standard' size bottle shrinks to 68 cl. Protest at such subterfuge by refusing to buy this wine – which may appear to be good value but is a deception.

When you see that a bottle contains 75 cl (the volume that the Common Market hope to institute in the near future, and some countries already insist upon), you will almost certainly be looking at a bottle containing superior wine.

So when you come to compare costs, that extra 5 cl has not only monetary but quality significance, too – not to mention the extra sips and almost a free bottle's-worth when the wine is bought by the case.

Other bottles may contain much smaller or larger quantities. As their volumes are usually related to halves or multiples of litres, comparison of price is easier – for the mathematically inclined.

In the larger volumes, the quality of the wine will usually be in the 'ordinary' class.

Magnums (two bottle's-worth) and greater sizes of fine clarets, Burgundies and Champagnes are the exception. Their larger capacities even help to improve the wine in the bottle.

ALCOHOL CONTENT

The labels of fine wines often omit to tell us the alcoholic degree of the contents. Those on cheaper wines are more obliging. But the alcohol content is important.

Higher alcohol levels tend to preserve the wine over longer periods – opened or unopened. Then, you may feel you are getting better value for stronger wine. Or you may want your tipple to go to your head (or someone else's) in rapid time.

Some light German wines are fine for quaffing on a hot summer's day – if served cold and, preferably, outside. They may contain not much more than 8 percent alcohol.

Liebfraumilchs are in the 9 to 10 percent bracket.

Standard white and red wines are usually 11 or 11.5 percent. Some reds go to 12 percent and even higher.

Hungarian white wines are usually 12 percent – high for a swilling wine. So watch them. Or do as the Hungarians do – add soda water.

The Americans, ever mindful of the relationship between ingested products and health, have now produced a 'de-alcoholized' white wine – Masson Light. Whereas this Californian wine would normally have held 10 percent alcohol, it now contains but 0.5 percent. Launched on the English market in the south-east, its cost, for 75 cl, is in the (£−2) range. **Sainsbury's** have it. They also offer Jung's de-alcoholized white wine (£−2), as do Peter Dominic, who also sell the red (£−2) and a German sparkler, Schloss Boosenberg (£2.50−3). **Safeway** offer alcohol-free Eisberg (£−2).

Others are bound to follow this trend, as there is, surely, a real demand for a drinkable, alcohol-free wine for those car-drivers who are alone or without an abstaining partner.

CORKS, CAPSULES AND BRANDS

Wine bottles generally have a capsule to cover the top of the neck. This adorning material can be of wax, tin-lead, plastic, tinfoil and, perhaps, other substances. They prevent you from seeing any moulds (quite all right) that might have formed on the cork, and stop the mice and weevils from enjoying a tasty, marinated-cork meal.

Tin-lead capsules are, by tradition, coverings for the best wines. As a wine purist, I like to see them used. But, as I lean toward the school of thought that we might be ingesting too many poisons for our own good, I'm frightened by them. After all, if marksmen can die from eating too many shot in game, and swans from consuming fishermen's lead weights, then those of us who have poured much wine from bottle openings encrusted with deteriorating tin-lead capsule material, must have one foot in the grave.

So when you cut off the top of one of these capsules (by running a blade along the upper shelf of the collar on the bottle neck), take extra care to clean the glass before and after extracting the cork. Using a damp piece of absorbent kitchen paper before extracting the cork, and a dry piece to follow, will do the trick.

Beside the reasons I gave for capsuling bottles, there is another that is seldom considered. Take a capsuled bottle. Cut around the top and discard the disc. Draw the cork. Pour some of the wine and, by controlled error, touch the rim of the wine glass with the capsuled bottle-neck. There will be a dullish noise and no damage done. If you tear away the entire capsule and do the same, you may well take a chip out of the rim of your glass.

Wines that a winemaker expects to be laid down will sport a long cork of good quality. At the other extreme, the quick-in-and-out boys will bung in the shortest cork obtainable. This may now often be an agglomerated one – that resin-bonded mixture of cork granules.

Good corks will have few holes or visible imperfections in them. And, as these constitute a considerable added expense to the bottler/winemaker, they will be a confirmation of wine quality.

The French often deceive us. Some of their corks may look perfect. On closer examination you will find that the holes have been covered over with a 'filler'. So, inside this outer skin, the cork may be almost as porous to air and wine as a visibly bad one.

A bad cork may spoil the wine by imparting a cork flavour to it (not always entirely unpleasant). But the expression 'corked' is now often used to indicate that the wine is 'off' in some way.

Plastic stoppers are seen in ever-increasing numbers – especially favoured for sparkling wines.

If a winemaker is really proud of his product, of his skills and of the origin of his wine, he may show it by branding his corks with the château name – and even the vintage year. When you draw one of these corks you can be fairly sure that something good will follow. An established and well-reputed wine merchant or négociant (dealer) will do the same (Berry Bros & Rudd or Louis Latour, etc.).

A winemaker who has less confidence in himself and his product, will use pre-branded corks that may say (in the lingo of the country) 'Bottled in Italy' or wherever, or 'Bottled in Our Cellars' and such-like. Wines held in by such corks may then be bought from the maker or bottler and have any label stuck to the bottle that a merchant thinks will help to sell the wine.

The Common Market wants all bottlers to brand their corks with a code number (G.B. bottlers use a W followed by four figures).

FLUCTUATING PRICES

As a rule, wine prices steadily rise. But sometimes they fall with a bang.

Claret drinkers will have noticed that there is a set pattern of exalted prices followed by a collapse. And those who lay down claret for future pleasure pounce at the opportune times.

The last collapse took place like this. A series of 'good' years turned up one after another. The drinkers of the world acquired a taste for superior wine, and bought lavishly. Producers became greedy. Prices rocketed.

The wine-buying public, not being mugs, then purchased from elsewhere. Unsold wine filled the cellars and warehouses. Room had to be made for new harvests, so the wine had to be sold quickly and cheaply.

In jumped those with an eye to such movements to fill their stores.

It's worth keeping an eye out for the next time that this might happen.

And wines from so-called 'off' years are usually much cheaper than those from the lauded vintages. Moreover, like great wines, they will quite often handsomely repay their owner if allowed to rest for some time before being consumed – with relish and with pride.

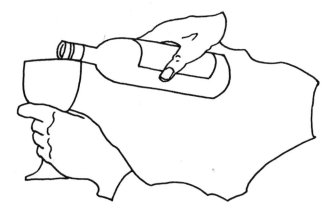

WINE SKULDUGGERY

There is lawlessness in the world of wine – as there is in most other businesses. Regulations are made not only in an attempt to ensure that wine quality is high but also to assure the buying public of that fact.

Various descriptions are allowed to be put onto the wine label to convince customers (before they buy it) that the wine in the bottle is absolutely genuine – and spiffing. Don't set too much store by these 'qualifications'. When certain laws are hard to enforce or unsatisfactory to producers, they may be ignored. It's rather like certain speed limits on the road.

I met a Frenchman who was forced to leave his vineyards in Algeria. He had set up again near Bordeaux.

Why, he asked himself, was his wine not as good as that of his neighbours? He would add sugar to the must if regulations allowed it. He was woken one night at vinification time by trucks on the road. These nocturnal rumblings were made by sugar tankers delivering to those less scrupulous.

Take it that we are all duped from time to time – wine merchants and customers alike.

Do you like what is in the glass? That's what counts. And governments do, actually, try to control quality and keep matters within bounds. Sometimes they fail.

Then there is the ticklish matter of 'additives'. An awful lot of noxious substances may pass through commercial wine on its way to our glasses. There is a move afoot to control or reduce these – certainly to make us more conscious of them. Two that sometimes remain in the wine are copper and sulphur. These are more noticeable after a wet summer's vintage.

Recent, shocking scandals concerning poisonous additives in wine are but some of the ever recurring disclosures of malpractice by blackguards.

It is an unfortunate fact of life that wine is easy to 'doctor'.

That this does not happen more often is because the wine trade is fundamentally an honest one, with most of those involved extremely proud of their product.

BOXES, TINS AND CARTONS

Wine boxes are here to stay. They are especially handy for a party or a swilling-picnic. But there are snags.

The wine does deteriorate fairly quickly – whatever we are told to the contrary. (Try to drink it up within two weeks of opening.) The wine inside is not always of the highest quality – and that in itself tells us something. The elderly have difficulty in opening the boxes – and even in operating the tap. And to invert the box by mistake when tampering with the tap allows air to enter and to spoil the wine more rapidly.

So, if the price is right (and they are not always 'best value') and the quality acceptable, they are fine in certain circumstances.

Canned wine is very handy and, unlike beer, seems not to suffer from contact with the tin's lining. The quality of the contents is about average, or slightly above. Tins may be deep-frozen. They can then help keep a picnic cool, and if still partly unfrozen when opened, give a cold, long-lasting drink that becomes weaker in alcohol as it progresses.

Small cartons may be tricky to open and inclined to spill. But the two glass-full size is acceptable – and handy for picnics and refrigeration. The quality of the wine, too, is sometimes above average.

The larger (one litre) cartons are acceptable only if their cheaper packaging substantially reduces the price. They are not easy to open, inclined to shoot their contents beyond the confines of the glass and are difficult to re-close well enough to protect the wine from spoilage and/or refrigerator smells.

Glass is, overall, the best container for wine. And it is cheap – but heavy and breakable.

OTHER SOURCES

Although supermarkets are often the best sources for wines, there are plenty of specialist wine merchants from whom to buy. These are not only in big cities. Some of the very best are housed quietly in country towns.

How to find them? A copy of *Decanter* or *Wine* magazine will contain advertisements from many. A post card to the ones that you fancy, to ask for their 'list', is all that is required. You will nearly always receive a courteous reply. And their catalogues are often brimming with information.

Some merchants have a licence to sell only by the case, though these case lots may often be made up with several different wines. Enthusiastic friends can club together to buy in this quantity.

The expertise of established, old-fashioned wine merchants is usually worth the extra cost of their wines. Do not be afraid of their 'smart' image. They actually *want* to sell wine to you.

The wine warehouses, where end-lots and mislabelled batches are sometimes acquired for quick sale at cheap prices, are well worth investigation. They sell top class wines as well.

But as with the several supermarkets, where splendid bargains are often to be found, the swift test and immediate return to stock up is most important.

Remember that wine clubs and societies are in it for the money. Their wines are often very interesting but seldom great bargains. They offer an easy method of buying wine for those hard pressed for 'searching time'. The larger ones are able to bulk-buy to cut costs. And their buyers exercise considerable skills on your behalf.

But start by seeking out the wines from supermarket shelves.

WHAT WINE WITH FOOD?

I think more baloney is written about what kind of wine you should drink with specific food than anything else in the business.

Let's face it, most of us are only too glad to have a single wine to accompany as many courses that come our way. If there are rules, they are there to be broken.

White wine is usually thought to be best with fish. The French don't always think so. They even drink Port before a meal and add red wine to their strawberries.

But certainly the tannin content of red wine tends to bring out a metallic taste in fish – to some tastes, enhancing it.

But if you are going the whole hog with several party wines, my feelings are these: drink before the meal should stimulate the digestive juices. Just-sweet, cool white wines can do this very successfully. Strong cocktails and fortified wines can worry the stomachs of some – as can spirits.

Serve dry white wines with fish and reds with meat – the stronger the meat the stronger the wine.

A soft, soothing and possibly sweet wine could then 'round things off' after the meal.

To leave wines on the table for guests to pour as they please is sensible and a fine mark of hospitality. The whites should, if possible, be kept in a cooler of some sort.

Otherwise you must decide on your wines with great self-assurance. No-one will respect you for doing otherwise.

FRANCE

BORDEAUX

We buy more wine from France than from anywhere else, and it varies in quality from the greatest obtainable in the world to over-sulphured, wine-lake plonk.

Let's tackle Bordeaux first. Claret – as Bordeaux is called – starts with an élite band of châteaux where the wine made is superlatively good and astronomically priced.

Even wine from the lowest orders of these 'classed' growths will seldom reach supermarket shelves – except, possibly, in poor years or under other names than their own. They can be dismissed from our minds, as they belong in the cellars of the rich, and more often than not, in the sale rooms – where they may change hands time and time again.

But lower down the scale come wines from the minor châteaux that, in a good year, can rival those of their far grander brethren, in terms of quality.

So the vintage year, in that respect, is important – remembering that howlers can be made in a good year and good wine in a bad one, by anyone.

And, as I have mentioned, a series of good years is even more important for the impecunious claret-lover, when any old 'Claret', 'Bordeaux', 'Bordeaux Superior' and the like may be both wonderful value and superb to drink.

Claret has a very special taste and style of its own. Moreover, good claret may be found at a reasonable price – when its rival from Burgundy seldom is.

To acquire a taste for Bordeaux wines will open up the door to a lifetime's enjoyment. But do not expect too much to start with if these wines are new to you. Buy some and 'build your way up'.

There are dry white wines from Bordeaux, too – especially from Entre Deux Mers. These are now often of the 'cold fermented' quality.

Of their sweet wines, Sauternes and Barsac are among the greatest. But look out for St Croix du Mont as a less cloying edition – and cheaper, too.

CHAMPAGNE

ALSACE

CHABLIS

THE LOIRE

BURGUNDY

BEAUJOLAIS

BORDEAUX

UPPER RHÔNE

LOWER RHÔNE
AND THE SOUTH

THE SOUTH WEST

BORDEAUX SELECTION

Waitrose often have a good claret (£2–2.50) and a selection of modestly priced château wines.

Unwins, though not cheap, are strong on the wines of Bordeaux. Try Bordeaux Rouge '83 (£3+) and Château La Peyrat (£3+).

Peter Dominic, with their top man conducting courses on wine in Bordeaux, are very reliable. Try their Claret (£2.50–3).

Davisons, too, have an excellent selection from minor châteaux. Their Bordeaux Rouge is (£2.50–3).

Carrefour have some imaginatively chosen bottles. Château Tour Prignac '83 (£2.50–3) is splendid quality/value. **Grandways** sell the same wine.

Budgen can pop in a surprisingly good bottle among their regulars. Try their claret (£2–2.50).

Eldridge Pope have a good range of clarets. Their Prince Louis Claret is good (£2.50–3).

Threshers sell Château de By (£3+). This comes from Bégadan – always a good part of the Médoc.

Stewarts sell Château Bel Air '83 and claret (£2.50–3).

Oddbins always choose well. Try their Château d'Archambeau '84, from Graves (£3+).

Townend offer an excellent white Bordeaux in Château Reynon '83 (£2.50–3) and a wonderful value claret in Château Brondeau '82 (£2.50–3). This is a wine to drink now or keep.

Dolamore's College Claret (£2–2.50) is always sound.

Hillards offer the Clos l'Eglise '82 Bordeaux Supérior (£2.50–3).

Presto's claret is a good bet (£2–2.50).

Fullers clarets are reasonably priced. They rather pride themselves on not being greedy with the finest.

Many shops sell sweet Sauternes and/or Barsac. Try **Sainsbury's** Clos St. Georges (£3+).

Walter Willson and **WM Low** sell sweet, white Bordeaux (£2–2.50).

Many others sell these sweet, white Bordeaux wines. There is not a lot between them.

British Home Stores offer a good claret (£2.50–3).

Tanners Wines sell their own claret (£2.50–3) – and it is very good.

BURGUNDY

Burgundy – the real stuff, like Nuits-Saint-Georges, Volnay and Montrachet – is expensive, and has always been so.

Burgundy is mainly a blended wine, bought from many small-volume growers and mixed by négociants (dealers) into a wine with a 'house' style (though more individuals are now dealing in their own product).

With much wine not originating at one château (as in Bordeaux, where it is grown, made and bottled on the premises), the whole process has lent itself to malpractice. In fact, much of our red Burgundy in the past has been 'fortified' with stronger stuff from sunnier climes.

Common Market regulations have actually had a bearing on the style of the wine that we import.

So, now that far more of it is 'real', we must accept that, as their climate is not good, the wines coming from the region are often thin and on the palish side.

But don't let that put you off Burgundy wines – though buying the fine ones is best left to the connoisseur who will find them in specialist wine merchants' shops.

A white Burgundy does sometimes turn up on supermarket wine shelves at a good price. It is Bourgogne Aligoté – the Burgundian's plonk. And it can be very good – especially when mixed with a slosh of blackcurrant liqueur.

BURGURDY SELECTION

Genuine Burgundy, with the exception of Beaujolais, being expensive, is not often a 'good buy' from supermarket shelves. The 'real stuff' is seldom below £3.

Morrisons and **Davisons** deal with the Burgundian wines of Georges Duboeuf (£3+) – always a reliable source.

Cullens sell the superb wines of Louis Jadot, as does **The Victoria Wine Company** (£3+).

Eldridge Pope have a very strong list of fine Burgundies.

Unwins sell a fine Aligoté (£3+).

Waitrose sell a lovely white Burgundy in Château de Meursault (£3+).

Peter Dominic's Geisweiler, Bourgogne Cuvée 18ème Siècle (£3+) will give you a taste of real Burgundy at a reasonable price.

Davisons sell a fine Côtes du Beaune Villages '84 (£3+). Their Mâcon Rouge is (£2.50–3).

One supermarket manages to provide a fair taste of Burgundy for under £3. It is **Safeway**.

Dickens Wine House offers a Mâcon Rouge (£2.50–3).

Tanners Wines sell an excellent Burgundy in Tanners Pinot Noir (£3+). It's the real thing – and won't break the bank.

THE LOIRE

Muscadet, a wine of fairly recent popularity, may be the first to come to mind when considering this region. It is a clean, dry and sometimes almost sharp wine. That is why it is so good when drunk with fish dishes.

The overall standard of this wine is high, so unless you are an expert, to buy a very expensive bottle will be a waste of your money. Look for bargains. And drink it cold.

Another very popular wine from this area, to be found on supermarket shelves, is Anjou Rosé. This has, until recently, catered for the sweeter toothed, British market – and still does to some extent. But as tastes develop toward drier wines, so Anjou Rosé toes the line. This move has tended to accentuate the taste of the grapes, so that much of it is now even more pleasant. If its past sweetness has put you off enjoying this wine, it could now be worth another try.

Other white wines that are fast becoming popular from this Loire region are Vouvray, Saumur, Touraine, Sauvignon Blanc de Touraine and Anjou.

A red worth investigating is Chinon. Unheard of in the UK a short time ago, this is now sometimes to be seen. And Anjou Rouge is a pleasingly fresh red.

The wines from the upper reaches of the Loire tend to become expensive and, thus, seldom reach supermarket shelves.

THE LOIRE SELECTION

Marks & Spencer offer a very good Anjou Rosé (£2.50–3).

Carrefour sell Chinon '84 (£2–2.50).

Sainsbury's stock a good Muscadet (£2.50–3).

Waitrose have a pleasing Vouvray, Château Moncontour '83 (£2.50–3).

Tesco offer a pleasant light red in Anjou Rouge (£–2).

Majestic Wine Warehouses sell Muscadet '84 and Chenin Blanc, both (£–2).

Cullens sell an excellent Muscadet (£2–2.50).

Foodrite specialize in Loire wines from Georges Rousseau. Their red Georges Rousseau (Cabernet Franc) sells for (£–2), and Loire white for the same price. For a sweet one, aim for their Coteaux du Layon (£2–2.50).

38

Though somewhat south of the Loire, **Lay** & **Wheeler** sell a most interesting Cabernet Rouge, Haut Poitou, for (£2.50–3).

Booths are an exception in that their reasonably priced Selection Auvigne (£2.50–3) hails from the more expensive upper reaches of the Loire.

Dolamore sell a good Muscadet (£−2).

Presto offer an excellent one. too (£2–2.50).

Fullers Muscadet sur Lie '84 (£2.50–3) is of the highest class.

And for a very special sweet Loire, try Moulin Touchais '55 or '69 (£3+) from **Tanners Wines** (not cheap, but extremely interesting).

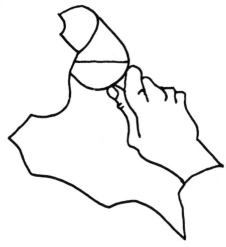

UPPER RHÔNE

The upper Rhône districts produce grand, deeply-coloured and robust wine.

They are fine to drink now with strongly flavoured stews and game. But they will also keep well and fine down to be wines with splendid class.

Some are expensive, it is true, but supermarket shelves are beginning to stock Hermitage, Crozes-Hermitage and Saint-Joseph. All are worth a try.

Don't bother too much about the vintage date.

UPPER RHÔNE SELECTION

The price of many of these wines is just around £3.

Safeway are expanding their selection of better Rhône wines. Their Saint Joseph '82 is lovely, and their Crozes-Hermitage '81 fine at (£3+).

Carrefour, too, are under our mark with Crozes-Hermitage (£2.50–3). **Fullers** '82 example is (£2.50–3) as well – as is the one from **Majestic Wine Warehouses**.

Morris's Wine Stores sell a fine St. Joseph '82, De Vallouit (£3+) at a reasonable price.

And **Waitrose** offer an excellent '82 Crozes-Hermitage, Caves des Clairmonts – as do **Davisons** (£3+). This wine has excellent quality/price value.

Townend sell the grand wines of Jaboulet and Chapoutier. Try their Crozes-Hermitage, Thalabert '82 (£3+).

Cullens sell a Jaboulet Isnard St. Joseph '80 (£3+).

Lay & Wheeler, who have a fine selection, offer Crozes-Hermitage Jaboulet (£3+).

LOWER RHÔNE AND THE SOUTH

From Châteauneuf du Pape, Gigondas and the surrounding areas come fine and full red wines.

Côtes du Rhône encompasses a large area and, although these wines are often rather 'pale', some are still robust and beautiful. They are certainly more distinctive than many of the sulphurous plonks offered from the southern (wine lake) region.

True Rhône wines sometimes have a pepperiness to them – like it or not. But any stating on the label that they contain the grape variety Syrah, will have more colour, taste and character.

Other names to look for in that part of the world are Tricastin, Ventoux and Luberon – all straightforward and seldom other than ordinary or just above. They are best drunk young.

Then, except for some worth-trying bottles from Provence, there is a belt of wine country cradling the Mediterranean coast, where bulk wines are made and where pockets of enthusiasts are up-grading their vine varieties – and, accordingly, their wine.

Bouches du Rhône can be strong and straightforward, as can

Costières du Gard, Languedoc and Corbières. Fitou and Minervois are usually a cut above the average. And because of its more stable climate, Roussillon is nearly always a fine choice.

LOWER RHÔNE AND THE SOUTH SELECTION

Tesco have a good example of Côtes du Rhône (£2.50–3) and a superb Châteauneuf du Pape, Les Arnevels (£3+).

Majestic Wine Warehouses are hunting grounds for wines from the lower Rhône and the south. Try their Côtes du Rhône (£–2) and Vacqueyras '83 (£3+).

Safeway sell many South of France wines, including a very good Fitou (£2–2.50).

The Victoria Wine Company offer good Côtes du Rhône (£2–2.50) and Côtes du Roussillon (£2.50–3).

Fine Fare and **City Grocers** offer the wines from this region. Try Côtes du Rhône '84 (£2.50–3).

Gough Brothers stock an exciting Syrah '83 Vin de Pays, from the Ardèche region (£2–2.50).

Oddbins, too, always have a good Côtes du Rhône, Bernard (£2–2.50) and a Minervois '84, Château de Donjon (£2–2.50).

Unwins sell an '84 Corbières (£2–2.50).

Bottoms Up offer a good Rhône in Côtes du Rhône Domaine Chartreuse '83 and '84 (£2.50–3).

Augustus Barnett and **Galleon** sell a well-selected Côtes du Roussillon Villages (£2–2.50).

Marks & Spencer offer a most pleasantly fresh Côtes du Rhône, Les Trois Oratoires '83 (£2.50–3) and a fine Châteauneuf du Pape '81 (£3+).

Carrefour sell fine and cheap litres of red from this region (£2–2.50). They are among the best of litre reds.

Littlewoods have an excellent selection of South of France wines – Corbières, Minervois, Coteaux du Languedoc and Côtes du Ventoux, (all £–2).

Threshers sell a good Fitou (£2–2.50) as do **Waitrose**.

Blayney Wines sell a sound Cabernet Sauvignon from the Aude (£2–2.50) and a superb Châteauneuf du Pape '83, La Pontificale (£3+).

Roberts/Cooper have a fine example of '83 Côtes du Rhône in Château de La Ramière (£2.50–3).

Morris's Wine Stores sell a good Côtes du Rhône Vacqueyras (£2.50–3).

And **Agnew Stores** sell a Côtes du Rhône at (£2–2.50). **Liquorsave, Winterschladen** and **North West Vintners** all sell an excellent Côtes du Roussillon (£–2).

And for a fine, good-value red, try **Fine Fare**'s Full Red (from Perpignon) (£–2). And their Côtes du Roussillon (£2.50–3) is excellent, too.

Lay & Wheeler's Côtes du Rhône, Château Grand Moulas '84 (£2.50–3), is a fine example.

Booths sell an interesting sweet Rivesaltes, Château de Jau (£3+).

Another sweet, 'pudding' wine from the region is Muscat Beaumes de Venise (£3+). This is a fashionable wine at present – and rightly so. It should be tried. **Bottoms Up, Carrefour, Davisons, Eldridge Pope, Tanners Wines, Lay & Wheeler, Dolamore** and many others have it.

Morrisons offer a most interesting Listel sur lie (£–2) from the very shores of the Mediterranean. They also have a Fitou (£2–2.50).

Walter Willson and **Thomas Patterson** offer the excellent Marsan & Natier Côtes du Rhône (£2–2.50).

Budgens sell more Fitou than other reds and consider it to be splendid quality/value (£2–2.50).

British Home Stores offer a Provence rosé – always a 'tougher' wine than those from the Loire. It is Château Montaud '83 (£3+).

BEAUJOLAIS

Although technically Burgundy, Beaujolais, because of the soil there and the sole use of the Gamay grape, is a wine on its own.

Almost half the production is now consumed as Nouveau, Primeur, Vin de l'Année or Nouveau Tirage de Primeur (all meaning much the same – 'new'). It must attain 9 percent alcohol.

Most of this comes from the southern part of the region.

Better wine, called Beaujolais-Villages (10 percent alcohol), comes from the north.

Also from this northern part come the 'special' wines of Saint Amour, Juliénas, Chénas, Moulin-à-Vent, Fleurie, Chiroubles, Morgon, Brouilly and Côte de Brouilly. These excellent wines will be made with more care and attention and are sold well after the Nouveau, ballyhoo rush.

The 'new' wine should be quaffed down soon after opening the bottle – before the delightful smells of the Gamay grape evaporate. For this reason they are best served at room temperature – though may be slightly chilled.

There are few better wines to accompany rich, Christmas food than Beaujolais Nouveau.

Most of this fresh wine is blended away from the region of production – to attain a 'house' style.

Do not set too much store by pronouncements on the success or failure of any one year. You may even prefer the product of a poor season.

BEAUJOLAIS SELECTION

Red Beaujolais is often a 'best seller' in wine shops and supermarkets – more so at 'Nouveau' time.

Morrisons stock the wines of Georges Duboeuf (£3+) – always ones to look for when seeking the best.

Davisons, too, sell Duboeuf wines (£3+).

Bottoms Up and **Peter Dominic** generally undercut other wine merchants with their Nouveau. And their edition may well be as good as most others.

The standard of Nouveau is high at **Arthur Cooper/Roberts** shops, as it is at **Waitrose, Safeway, Victoria Wine, Oddbins, Gough Brothers** and many others. Prices are generally (£2– 2.50 and £2.50–3).

Morris's Wine Stores sell excellent Beaujolais Villages, Pichet, (£3+).

And **Waitrose**'s Beaujolais Villages is usually very good, too (£2.50–3).

Beaujolais (£2–2.50) is a big seller at **Lo-Cost**.

Dickens Wine House sell a superb '83 Chiroubles (£3+).

CHABLIS

Chablis is a white wine that, when genuine and fine, is one of the greatest obtainable. But expect to pay a lot for the real thing.

The climate there is poor and the acreage small. It is said that the entire production of the region could not supply Paris alone with its needs. That's why you should not expect too much from those bottles in the lower price range.

CHABLIS SELECTION

Chablis at under our £3 cut-off mark must be treated with caution. These wines are generally (£3+).

Marks & Spencer offer a fine '84, as do **Waitrose, Sainsbury's** and **Tesco**.

Mellor & Patison and **The Vineyard** offer a splendid '83.

Majestic Wine Warehouses specialize in Chablis wines. They sell six different ones.

THE SOUTH-WEST

Between the Bordeaux region and the Pyrenées lies a charming backwater of France, from whence come some formidable red and delicate white wines. The region is well worth investigating – vinously and geographically.

One of the wines that makes a regular appearance on supermarket shelves is red Bergerac.

It is a cheaper relation of the better-known Bordeaux district nearby – but often great stuff for the price. It is a fine wine to accompany winter food.

Buzet red wine is sometimes seen, and Gaillac, too. And wine from Madiran and Cahors are known to appear. They are all worth trying – though Cahors can be a little 'inky' when young.

Should you have a taste for sweet wines, try Monbazillac and, especially, Jurançon Moelleux should you find one. These are a couple of very good, sweet wines to compare with Sauternes and Barsac, from the Bordeaux region.

THE SOUTH-WEST SELECTION

Unwins stock the red Cahors '82 (£2.50–3), and **Peter Dominic,** one for (£2–2.50).

Sainsbury's offer a good, red Buzet '82 (£2–2.50). Like most wines from this region, it would keep and soften. They also stock Gaillac in three litre boxes and 70 cl bottles of white Bergerac (£–2). The red is (£2–2.50).

Tesco sell a good, red Bergerac (£2–2.50), and **Asda,** an even cheaper one (£–2).

Bordeaux Direct have a fine selection from this part of France.

Waitrose sell excellent Buzet (£2–2.50), as do **Carrefour** (£2.50–3).

Lay & Wheeler sell a splendid value/quality, white Côtes de Gascogne, Colombard (£2–2.50), as do **Fullers** and **Bunches.**

Yes, these white Gascony wines do represent fine class/value at present. Seek them out where you can.

Waitrose offer a fine Jurançon sec (£2.50–3), as do **Tanners.**

Majestic Wine Warehouses stock Cépage Sauvignon from Bergerac (£2.50–3). This wine powerfully exhibits the taste of the Sauvignon Blanc grape.

ALSACE

Finally, from France, I pick out the wines of Alsace. And you should pick them, too. These, at last, are reaching a price range that justifies their inclusion on supermarket shelves.

The most striking is Gewurztztraminer (displaying the grape name on the label). A sip of this wine is a mouthful, so much taste seems to be concentrated into it. Gewurztztraminers vary in the density of their taste. So try around to find one to suit your palate. Then buy some more to keep.

Do not confuse this wine with Gewurztztraminers from else-where. Only the Alsatians seem to know how to make a wine in the grand style from this grape variety.

Sometimes you will find Alsace wines for sale that are made from other grape varieties. Each will have the name of this grape on the label. But do not expect them to be as pungent in taste as the Gewurztztraminer. Yet most are lovely wines.

Look for the grape varieties Riesling, Sylvaner, Pinot (Tokay) and Muscat – not, in this case, turned into the general run of sweet dessert wines, but a delicate one with just a hint of that delightful Muscatel taste.

ALSACE SELECTION

Peter Dominic sell the very fine Hugel Alsace wines. The Pinot Blanc is (£2.50–3) but the Riesling and Gewurztztraminers are above £3 (as one would expect). **Davisons** sell Hugel wines, too.

Tesco's Gewurztztraminer (£3+), and **Waitrose**'s Riesling and Gewurztztraminer are (£2.50–3) good.

Eldridge Pope stock a fine selection from the houses Dopff & Irion and Louis Sipp (£3+).

Lay & Wheeler start off their extensive range with Blanck's Sylvaner Reserve '84 (£3+).

Marks & Spencer sell a Riesling (£2.50–3), and **Sainsbury's** a Pinot Blanc (£2–2.50) and Sylvaner (£2.50–3) – as do **Oddbins** and **Bottoms Up** in the same price range.

Safeway offer a Sylvaner d'Alsace (£2–2.50).

GERMANY

Imports of German white wine increase year by year, and as much of it is Liebfraumilch, I will give this blended wine a chapter to itself.

As for the rest of the wines from Germany, they do represent very good value when compared with the equivalent in class from other countries.

Take it that most white wines (there are reds, too, but not often seen here) have a sweet side to them. That is, except for Trocken (dry) and Halbtrocken (half dry).

Then there is a grading system that states clearly on the bottle what the quality is of the wine inside it.

The key words to look for here are these:

Bereich = in the district of...

Tafelwein = table wine.

Deutcher Tafelwein = table wine made only from German grapes.

Deutcher Landwein = Special German table wine – and will state the region from whence it comes.

Now we move up a step to:

Qualitätswein = Class wine.

But *Qualitätswein bA* (*QbA*) is still an everyday wine from a specific region.

Qualitätswein mit Pradikat = Wine with special distinction. And these distinctions are, in ascending order: *Kabinet*, *Spätlese*, *Auslese*, *Beerenauslese*, *Eiswein* and *Trocken-beerenauslese*.

To elucidate on these last catagories:

Kabinet = light and drier than the rest.

Spätlese = late harvest = more flavour.

Auslese = wine made from very ripe grapes = sweeter wine.

Beerenauslese = rare, rich and sweet = a dessert wine.

Eiswein = syrupy sweet wine which would last for sixty years or more to be at its best. It is made from frozen grapes.

Trockenbeerenauslese = wine made from almost raisin-dry grapes (the Trocken bit does not mean 'dry' wine but that it has been made with 'dry' grapes).

47

Hock, generally in brown bottles, will be sweeter than Mosel, in green bottles.

The name of the district of production, printed on German wine labels, will give you some idea of the wine inside.

I say 'some idea' because each 'schloss' may produce up to nine styles of wine each year – not to mention that the wine will vary from year to year.

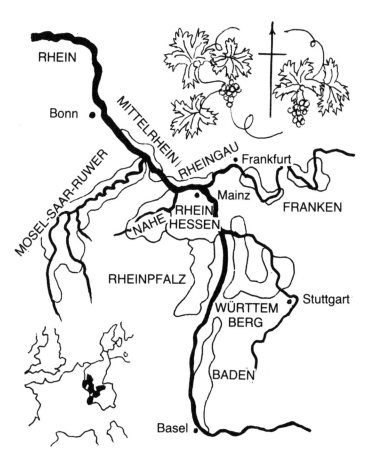

GERMAN WINE REGIONS

Very little wine reaches us from the regions of Ahr and Hessische Bergstrasse, as most of it is consumed locally.

Baden wine, from the Black Forest region, is thought to be the fullest – as it comes from Germany's most southerly, and warmest, vineyard area.

Würtemberg produces mainly red wines. Aim for the quaffably pleasant examples made from the Trollinger grape.

The Rheinpfalz region produces the most wine, thought to be the richest. The finer wines come from the more northerly parts.

Rheinhessen is the original home ground of Liebfraumilch (see later). The wine from this area is generally light, flowery and easy to drink. Bereich Nierstein is one of them.

Wines from Nahe can relate to those of Mosel to the west or Rheinhessen to the east. They might be classed, in general terms, as Liebfraumilchs with more acidity.

Rheingau produces the classic wines of Germany. Made from the great Riesling grape, they are full, fruity wines with acidity. Be prepared to pay more for them – and they are usually well worth it.

Franken wines are very earthy. Offered in flagon-shaped bottles, they are most distinctive with their full and gutsy flavours.

Rhein maidens hold sway from the picturesque, medieval castles of Mittelrhein. They either drink a lot of their wine themselves, or seduce their menfolk with so much, that it seldom reaches our supermarket shelves. And it really is rather a seductive wine.

From the river banks of Mosel-Saar-Ruwer come wines known as Mosels (Piesporter from Bereich Bernkastel is a well-known one).

They have that delightful balance that makes them seem to be both sweet and dry at the same time.

GERMAN WINE SELECTION

Asda sell an Auslese, made from the Ortega grape, that is excellent – Nussdorfer Bischofskreuz '83 (£2.50–3).

Morrisons have a good list of German wines.

Marks & Spencer sell a pleasant Mosel Riesling (£2–2.50).

Bejam's customers buy a great deal of Dr. Willkomm's wine in three-litre boxes.

The Victoria Wine Company sell an excellent Morio Muskat by the litre (£3+). It's a good party wine.

Waitrose have a limited selection of German wines, but they are very well chosen, and their cheap, Hock Tafelwein is quite excellent (£–2).

Fine Fare sell these wines at modest prices. Try their Piesporter Michelberg (£2.50–3).

A popular sweet wine, in Binger St. Rochus Auslese (£3+), is to be found in **Agnew Stores**.

Booths Nierstein Spiegleberg '83 (£2–2.50) is well worth a try.

Wm Low/Lowfreeze find their Niersteiner Berncastle (£2–2.50) to be a great seller.

Julian Flook's Longnicher Probsberg Kabinet '84 Mosel, at (£2.50–3) is excellent.

Drew and **Cellar 5** think very highly of their Wiltinger Scharzberg Kabinet and Piesporter (£2.50–3).

Besant's Niersteiner is (£–2).

Blayney Wines offer a fair Mosel Tafelwein (£–2).

And **Budgen**'s Niersteiner Gutes Domtal is (£–2).

Hillards Niersteiner is (£–2).

Liquorsave and **Winterschladen**'s Piesporter is (£2–2.50).

Bottoms Up sell Bereich Johannisberg Riesling '83 (£2.50–3).

Littlewood's Piesporter Michelsberg is (£2–2.50).

Presto sell Tafelwein and Hock (£–2).

Shoppers Paradise offer their Mosel Deutcher Tafelwein at (£–2).

Spar's Mosel Tafelwein and their Piesporter are reasonably priced.

Tates Piesporter is (£2–2.50).

Carrefour sell Halgarten's Niersteiner Gutes Domtal '84 at (£2–2.50).

And **Co-Op** offer a very good Lohingrin Bereich Nierstein (£2–2.50).

Dolamore's College Hock costs (£2–2.50).

And **Dickens Wine House** sell an excellent Berncastler Kurfurslay, as well as its Trocken (dry) version, for (£–2).

Thresher's Hock and Mosel are (£2–2.50).

Walter Willson sell their Piesporter for (£2–2.50).

Tanners sell an '82 Franken wine – Wurzburger Stein Riesling Kabinet (£3+).

And **Townend** offer Baden Prince (£2–2.50) and another Baden wine, Ortenau Riesling '83 (£2.50–3).

Foodrite sell Englehof's Moselblumchen (£2–2.50).

Deinhard German wines have class, style and reliability.

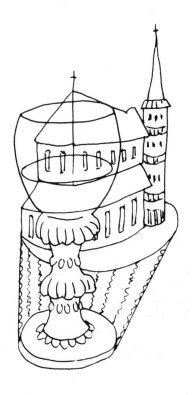

LIEBFRAUMILCH

Being by far the nation's most popular white wine, Liebfraumilch commands a section to itself.

When the Romans reached Worms, in Germany, they found that the wine made there was delicious and more delicate than the existing litre, daily ration wine to which their legionnaires were entitled. So they fostered the wine industry to reduce the load on their lines of supply.

The Dark Ages came and went, and wine continued to be made in that same area.

In medieval times, monks built a church there and called it the Liebfrauenkirch (Church of Our Lady). They, too, tended the vines.

In the eighteenth century, an Englishman, called Maximillion Mission, returned home from Worms and wrote a book. He referred to the wine as being so delicious that the monks thought it to be as sweet as the milk from the Holy Virgin. And that was the first record of the name Liebfrau(en)milch used as a description of this wine.

Since then, however, the name has been bastardized to the extent that at one time most of the wine from Germany was referred to as Liebfraumilch — and much of that came from Austria and Alsace.

Rules have now tightened up a bit, and, at present, they stand thus:

'The wine should have a must weight of 60 Oe., be a quality German wine, be tested by the State to ensure and maintain that quality, be in the medium/sweet direction and be made mainly from the grape varieties Riesling, Silvaner and Muller Thurgau.'

Which all comes to mean that the wine is a blend of German wine that can be altered according to prevailing market forces.

Surprisingly enough, although this white wine is our nation's favourite, the Germans hardly touch a drop of it.

And as we, in Great Britain, become a nation of wine drinkers so, like such nations before us, the initial taste for sweetish wines gives way to that for drier ones. Liebfraumilch is becoming drier.

There is no doubt that this wine is a sound one, made in acceptable forms to meet most tastes. And in considering what I have just written, the cheapest may be the best for you. Remember that advertising costs money – and must be paid for by you, the buyer. Start with the ones that cost least. Then work your way up until you find a pleasing one.

Although the basic cost of Liebfraumilch may rise (with the usual moanings and dire predictions), the wine merchants will do their best to keep the price low for their consumers. Liebfraumilch drinkers are 'tied' drinkers. And should the price of a bottle rise to a degree where those consumers start to buy from the world of wines outside, they may never return to their first love. And the sellers of our most popular wine are fully aware that their enormous trade would then suffer.

Some of the best-known brands of Liebfraumilch are Blue Nun, Black Tower, Crown of Crowns and Goldener Oktober. All keep up a high standard of quality.

Being our most popular wine, you may be sure that all wine shops and supermarkets will stock Liebfraumilch. If they are *very* smart, they might call it Sylvaner/Muller Thurgau (Hock).

It seems that with every harvest we hear that the price of our 'favourite' will rise. Yet merchants have managed to keep the cost down to attractive and sensible levels – often below £2 and sometimes a bit above. Let's hope it continues.

LIEBFRAUMILCH SELECTION

Asda's Liebfraumilch is a best-seller, as is **Morrisons**.

Colman's boxed Liebfraumilch (£3+) is generally available and well worth a try.

Marks & Spencer specialize in this wine, as do **Bejam**.

For **Tesco** it is a best-seller, as it is, or nearly so, with **Arthur Cooper/Roberts, Unwins, Peter Dominic, Liptons, Presto, Hintons, Spar, Crispins, Gateway, International, Co-Op, Carrefour, British Home Stores, Waitrose, Sainsbury's, Budgen, Shoppers Paradise, Gough Brothers, Littlewoods, Grandways, Lalani's, Threshers** (who sell seven different kinds), **Arthur Rackham, Majestic Wine Warehouses, Safeway, Victoria Wine, Cullens, Fine Fare, Oddbins, Davisons, Augustus Barnett, Galleon, Hillards, Besant, Bottoms Up, Yates, Blayney Wines, Winterschladen, City Grocers, Gal-**

braith, Foodrite, Le Riche's, Morris's Wine Stores, Saverite, VG, Stewarts, Tates, Townend, Wm Low, Lowfreeze, Booths, Lo-Cost, Walter Willson, Agnews, Mace Line, Airey's Wine Stores, Dickens Wine House, Fullers, Bunches, Europa Foods, **Julian Flook** (a special one), **James Mellor Wines, Normans, Mellor & Patison, The Vineyard, Drew, Cellar 5, Bottles, Queen's Cellars, John Sarson, Rutland Vintners, G.B. Wines, Tanners Wines**... I'm out of breath.

EUROBLENDS

Because this blend of various wines from the European community is sometimes sold under the guise of 'German' wine (with Gothic lettering), it should not be despised – or mistaken for German wine. Price is usually much in its favour, and the blenders can sometimes come up with a very pleasant mix.

And, after all, from the smartest Bordeaux châteaux (where they blend the wine from several of their own-grown varieties) to 'litre' wine, to Liebfraumilch and onwards, wine is, unless named on the label as a varietal (only one grape mentioned), blended wine. So why not Euroblend it from 'cheap' areas to keep the cost down for those who cannot afford more? Pay no heed to the snobbish attitudes of those who would decry it.

EUROBLEND SELECTION

Oddbins sell an excellent Euroblend in Drathen Tafelwein (£−2).

The cartons of Domkellerstolz (£2−2.50) and three litre boxes of Dr. Willkomm's blend are best-sellers at **Bejam**.

Stewarts sell a lot of Weinkeller Gold (£−2).

Morrisons offer a good brew in Pfeiffer Tafelwein (£−2).

Agnew's Sortima Tafelwein (£−2) is popular.

Lo-Cost's Winzerschoppen (£−2) is so good that it even outsells Liebfraumilch.

Dolomore offer a Tafelwein (£−2).

Spar sell a great deal of Siebrand Winzerschoppen (£−2).

Julian Flook offers St. Helena (£−2).

Sainsbury's sell a blend for (£−2).

Dickens Wine House sensibly call theirs Europa (£−2).

James Mellor Wines sell litres of their 'House Wine' for (£2.50−3).

The Victoria Wine Company have Kronen Tafelwein (£−2).

Drew and Cellar 5 sell the most successful Grunnengold (£−2).

Blayney Wines offer their Klosterschoppen blend (£−2).

Tanners Wines stock Sonnenstubchen Tafelwein (£−2).

You see what I mean by all the 'Germanic' labelling. There is no need to hide this perfectly legitimate, multi-country blend beneath the decorative skirts of Germany.

Presto Tafelwein's price makes it extremely popular (£−2).

John Sarson, Bottles, G.B. Wines, Queen's Cellars and **Rutland Vintners** sell Gold Vine (£−2).

Sherston Wine Company offer two Euroblends. The dry one is St. Urban Tropfchen (£−2) and the medium one, Kirschmeister (£−2).

Majestic Wine Warehouses sell Winzerkrone (£−2).

SPAIN

WHITES AND REDS

From Spain come ordinary, strong, rough plonks and some of the finest wines available. And as vinification methods improve, there will be fewer of those rough-'uns.

The areas in which to look for the best are Rioja, Penedes and Navarra. These regions can produce wines of splendid quality for the price asked.

Red Rioja prices are rising, but bargains are always to be found. Aim for the 'Crianza' quality. This will be printed in a scroll at the top of the back label. It may say Vino de Crianza. What this means is that the wine has had some age in old oak casks and further age in bottle before being sold. Below this quality you may see C.V.C. printed on the back label (meaning mixed vintages). Or there may be a decorative picture of peasant vintagers or shields with no words of encouragement. This will mean much the same thing.

Above Crianza quality come Reserva and Gran Reserva. These wines have more, and yet more, oak and bottle age. And, in this ageing, they will lose a lot of their fresh fruitiness, fine down, become paler and browner, and, sometimes take on a touch of bitterness. They are very special wines – very 'different'.

The whites from Rioja that appear on our shelves will probably be of the cold fermentation quality – clean, fresh, lemony, etc. (see chapter on cold fermentation). If you find one of the Crianza quality, buy it. This will be a well-above-average white wine.

Red Penedes wines are well worth a try. The whites, with an exception or two, will probably be clean, fresh, lemony, etc.

The quality of wine from other areas of Spain, too, is steadily rising, so look out for them.

SPANISH WINE SELECTION

Sherston Wine Company specialize in Spanish wines and have a fine collection. Look for Muga and Marques de Murietta Riojas (£3+).

Majestic Wine Warehouses often have bargains – like Cune's red Rioja (£2.50–3), Torres Coronas '81 (red) (£2.50–3) and one of the best white Riojas, Monopole '82 (£3+).

Bottoms Up are especially strong on the wines of Rioja. They offer a choice of 36 or more. Try Senorio de los Llanos Gran Reserva (£3+).

Tesco sell a very good and cheap Rioja, Vina Lanaga (£2–2.50) and Gran Feudo Navarra (£–2).

Fine Fare's Rioja is excellent value (£2–2.50), and their quality/value Spanish dry white and red (£–2) is hard to beat.

Peter Dominic offer Spanish white and red (–2), Lagunilla Rioja (£2.50–3) and Domecq Domain Rioja (£3+).

Asda have some interesting Spanish wine, including a white from Alella, Domain Manaut (£2.50–3). They offer the Don Cortez range, too.

Waitrose stock the good, white, Olarra Rioja (£3+), and that excellent red Navarra, Gran Feudo (£2–2.50).

Carrefour sell a good Rioja, Paternina '76 and Tres Torres '81 red (£2.50–3).

Gateway offer their own-label Spanish red and white from Valencia (£–2).

Littlewoods sell a great deal of their bargain wine from Valencia, Tarona (£–2).

Threshers sell Corrida (£–2) and five kinds of Rioja. Try their Domecq's Vina Eguia '81 (£2.50–3) and Marques de Caceres '81 (£3+).

The Victoria Wine Company stock their Don Cortez range (£–2) and Banda Azul Rioja (£2.50–3).

Marks & Spencer sell their fine litre bottles of Rioja Romeral and its even better Gran Reserva Rioja, Marques del Romeral (£3+).

And **Townend** sell a good Rioja in a hessian sack. It is Arpillera (£2–2.50).

Walter Willson sell the Don Cortez range (£–2).

Lo-Cost, too, sell a lot of this wine.

Safeway's Raimat Abadia is one of Spain's best red wines – oaky and fruity (**The Victoria Wine Company** sell it, too). And their Moscatel de Valencia (£2–2.50) is a splendidly sweet and fruity 'pudding' wine.

Barrett may still have some Conde Bel '77 or '78 Rioja (£–2) left.

Fine Fare and **City Grocers** offer Rioja Bodegas Franco Espanolas '82 (£2–2.50) and a dry Spanish white and red (£–2).

Oddbins offer red '82 Rioja Añares (£2.50–3). This is very good.

Augustus Barnett and **Galleon** sell that excellent Rioja, Campo Viejo (£2.50–3) and the good value Donnilla (£–2).

SPANISH SHERRY

Sherry, a name and drink once on everyone's lips, is passing through the doldrums of an over-abundance of cheap and inferior wine on the market. Cycles in wine tastes do happen, and sherry must rise in people's esteem once more. It is still good value wine, and there are excellent ones for sale. I believe that this wine is gaining in popularity as an aperitif.

The very finest are grand wines, indeed. But these are usually too expensive to find their way onto supermarket shelves – though some are now appearing.

SPANISH SHERRY SELECTION

Sherries and Montillas are obtainable from nearly every supermarket and wine shop.

Tesco are setting the style by introducing some fine sherries to extend their existing range. At (£2.50–3), their Premium Range – especially the Amontillado – is excellent.

Sainsbury's sherries also cost (£2.50–3). Try their Manzanilla (very dry).

Waitrose sell a good Barbadillo, dry, Manzanilla (£3+).

The Dominicus range from **Peter Dominic** and **Bottoms Up** is good (£2.50–3).

Besant sell the popular Mackenzie Perla (£2–2.50).

Fine Fare offer litres of Mandola or their own brand (£2.50–3).

Augustus Barnett sell William & Humbert Dry Sack (£3+).

Davisons offer their Don Avides (£2.50–3).

For a lovely sweet sherry, try **Lay & Wheeler**'s Oloroso Especial Hildago (£3+).

Tates sell more Montilla (£2–2.50) than sherry.

Croft Particular (£3+) goes down well at **Agnew Stores**.

Townend sell the excellent range of Wisdom & Warter sherries (£2–2.50).

Booths offer their own brand at (£2.50–3).

Lo-Cost sell the Domecq range (£2.50–3).

Budgens own label sells at (£2.50–3).

Presto sell a good Presto sherry (£2.50–3) and the Gonzales Byass Elegante range (£3+).

The Domecq sherries are available at **Unwins** (£2.50–3).

And Harvey's Bristol Cream (£3+) is one of the most popular of all sherries at Christmas time. It is available throughout the country.

In Bristol, too, **Julian Flook**'s Howells of Bristol range is excellent (£2.50–3).

Drew and **Cellar 5** find their Five Cellars brand to be most popular (£2.50–3).

Tanners Wines offer their own, very acceptable, brand (£2.50–3).

John Sarson Wines, G.B. Wines, Queen's Cellars, Bottles and **Rutland Vintners** all sell the popular and excellent brand Frontera (£3+).

Garvey, one of the finest sherry 'houses' sell a splendid Fino called San Patricio (£3+). It is stocked by **Majestic** and **Whynot Warehouses, Sherston Wine Company** and some branches of **Peatling and Cawdren**. It is also sold in half bottles as fine wines, such as these, tend to deteriorate fairly quickly.

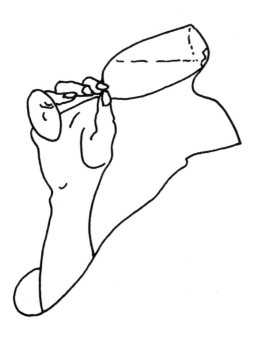

PORTUGAL AND MADEIRA

Port manufacturers are marketers par excellence. Their wares are easily obtainable from supermarket shelves – more so at Christmas time.

Other Portuguese wines, except for Madeira, Vinho Verde, Dão and Mateus wines, are only just beginning to enter the international, hard-sell arena. Look out for them – especially those from Bairrada and Douro.

Let's start with port. Leaving aside white port, which has not yet found a firm place in our affections, we should start with the most popular port of all – Ruby.

The grapes for this have not reached the quality needed for the higher grades. Yet it has had some years in cask and is fortified, as are all ports, with brandy. It constitutes the main part of port sales in this country.

After fine port has been carefully blended and has had six to forty or more years in cask, it takes on a light, browny colour. This is Tawny port. The real thing is very special and gives one the impression of being delicate, yet high in alcohol.

Now comes Late Bottled (L.B.), Late Bottled Vintage (L.B.V.), Vintage Character, Vintage Style, Founder's Reserve, Directors' Bin (or Choice), Bin 27 (or such), Crusted, Chairman's Choice (or Bin), Special Reserve, etc. What do they all mean?

These are made with the same quality, fortified, top grade wine as is used for vintage port. It has been bottled after four to six years in cask – when it will have thrown off its impurities. It is ready to drink right away – without the tedium and ritual of decanting. And it is a very good substitute for vintage port.

Vintage Port is made from the best quality grapes. When fermentation has produced about 8 percent alcohol, brandy is added (435 litres of wine + 115 litres of spirit = 1 Pipe). This remains in cask for 22 to 31 months, and is then bottled. Now it rests in cellars for many years until ready to drink. Then the wine must be decanted off the 'crust' lying in the bottle. It will last for several days in its decanter without deteriorating.

Dão is a woody red wine that is generally sold in super-markets at a price well below its true value. This tough wine goes well with game. And it will keep well, too.

Mateus wines, and their equivalent in flagons, are slightly prickly, sweetish wines, blended very successfully for the British market.

Vinho Verde is a young, fresh wine that tickles the tongue with minute bubbles. It is a refreshing, low-alcohol wine and well worth a try – especially if drunk cold on a hot summer's day. It has quite a strong character of its own.

PORT SELECTION (£3+)

Most wine departments sell Ruby port, if not Tawny, Vintage Character and Vintage. All are above our £3 cut-off mark- except one. I found Roze's Port at **Barrett**. But I'm sure that would have gone by now.

Gough Brothers sell Graham's Late Bottled Vintage '79, always one of my favourites.

The Victoria Wine Company offer Cockburn's Late Bottled '80, Noval and Taylor's '79.

Specialist, old-fashioned wine merchants, like **Lay & Wheeler, Tanners, John Sarson** and **Eldridge Pope** (who sell half bottles, too), will stock the widest selection of Vintage Port for those wishing to delve further into the subject.

Oddbins sell a fine Old Vintage Character Port called Guimareans. They also stock the Late Bottled Vintage Ports of Graham's and Dow's.

Tanners Wines own Patrono Fine Old Ruby is very popular.

Arthur Rackham sell the excellent Late Bottled Vintage '79 from Sandeman.

James Mellor Wines, Mellor & Patison and **The Vineyard** offer a most comprehensive range of vintage port.

Asda sell another good Late Bottled Vintage '79 – Dow.

Bunches offer an interesting port in Royal Oporto '82.

Threshers sell LBV Ferreira '80.

Sainsbury's port is to be recommended.

Noval port is to be found at **Airey's Wine Stores**.

Graham's LBV '78 can be found at **Majestic Wine Warehouses.**

Townend sell their Sportsman, and **Booths** their own brand Vintage Character.

Budgens offer Seagram's Founders Reserve.

Presto sell a good Ruby and **Dolamore** their College Port.

Carrefour offer Noval LB, Cockburn's, Sandeman's and Croft's.

Yates Brothers Limited specialize in shipping their own port. Their vintage style Old Bismark port is excellent as is their Velhissimo (Old Tawny).

MADEIRA SELECTION (£3+)

Madeiras, too, are above the (£3+) range. Among the most popular are Blandy's, Donaldson, Rutherford & Miles, Henriques & Henriques, Cossart Gordon and Leacock.

Peter Dominic sell Blandy's Duke of ... range – as do **Bottoms Up.**

British Home Stores stock Cossart Gordon's Malmsey.

Sainsbury's sell their own brand.

Lay & Wheeler offer the Cossart Gordon range.

And **Tanners** not only sell the Cossart Gordon range, but Rutherford & Miles and Blandy's as well.

Davisons offer The Duke of Clarence Malmsey.

Dolamore sell their own Madeira, and **Eldridge Pope**, the Madieras from Rutherford & Miles.

Madeiras, like Ports, are liable to turn up in many shops and supermarkets at Christmas time when their shelf-space will have been better used throughout the year.

PORTUGUESE WINE SELECTION

Sainsbury's offer an excellent, full, red wine in Quinta da Bacalhoa (£3+).

Waitrose, too, have a good one in Tinto da Anfora '81 (£2.50–3). They also stock Dão '76 (£2–2.50).

Tesco has Dão (£2–2.50). In fact, many wine outlets sell this 'meaty' wine at about that price.

Agnew Stores offer Mateus Rosé and Mateus white (£2.50–3). Their Vinho Verde is (£2–2.50). This is about the price range for these popular wines throughout the land.

Oddbins offer a red Quinta do Convento '76, from Fonseca (£2–2.50).

Threshers sell a Dão, called Dom Ferraz (£2–2.50), and they sell a white Dom Ferraz, too (£2–2.50).

Most stores will sell the Mateus range and many, a Vinho Verde.

ITALY

So many different wines come from Italy that we can mention but a sample. But why *are* there relatively so few on our supermarket shelves?

Dealers in the trade complain that consistency is lacking. And with the same wine varying so much in quality, it is difficult for them to establish a market. But I hear that matters are improving all the time.

Chianti is made from both red and white grapes. Most supermarkets sell this 'clean' wine.

Another range of wines that has recently made an appearance comes from the Alto Adige (South Tyrol). The vineyards from which they come are among the highest in Europe – some above 3,000 feet. The mountain air is reflected in the wine. They have a charm – a delicacy – about them.

Valpolicella is another wine often to be seen on our supermarket shelves. At its best it is superbly fresh and quaffable. At its worst, it is ordinary. So this is a wine to sample before you buy too much at one time. Also from near Verona comes delicious, white Soave.

Now we come to the classy wines of Piedemont in north-west Italy.

Dolcetto might be described as sweeter Beaujolais Nouveau. Both it and Nebbiolo d' Alba are made to the producers specifications. They are swilling wines.

Barbera is an inky, dark wine that goes well with garlicky stews. Bardolino is a light, fresh red.

Both Barbaresco and Barolo are made from the classic Nebbiolo grape variety. Barbaresco is the 'easier' of these great wines, but Barolo is king – and needs many years to reach its exalted and rightful stature.

White and red Lambrusco now appear on supermarket shelves. They are specialist, fun wines – both being sweet, fruity and fizzy – and *very* popular.

From near Rome, come those crystal clear Frascatis that are such ideal summer wines. They go very well with Chinese food.

And from the Veneto (a huge area inland from Venice) come some truly excellent wines.

Marsala, from Sicily, could be more popular as an aperitif wine.

Orvieto turns up in both its sweet and dry style – they should be tried.

And for a sweet wine, try Moscato Naturale d'Asti. This delicious, still Muscatel wine should be drunk young.

Mention must be made of Italy's large Mediterranean island of Sardinia. For it is from here that Waitrose are now obtaining their excellent carafe wines.

ITALIAN WINE SELECTION

Tesco have an Orvieto (£2−2.50), and, from the South Tyrol, a Lago di Caldaro (£−2), a Valdadige Bianco (£−2) and a very pleasant Soave (£−2). Try their red Barbera (£−2), and especially their red Lambrusco di Sorbara (£−2).

Waitrose sell a delicate Gewurtztraminer (£3+) from Alto Adige, a red Venegazzu '80 from the Veneto and an '84 Valpolicella (£−2). Their Corsican carafe white and red (£2−2.50 a litre) would be hard to beat as party wines. Try their Lambrusco (£2−2.50).

Sainsbury's stock red Raboso del Veneto (£−2), a white Soave (£−2), Sicilian Tonino (£−2) and Lambrusco (£−2).

Oddbins specialize in Italian wines (they stock about 50). Their Chianti is (£2−2.50), Barbera d' Asti '83 (£2.50−3) and Soave Fabiano (£−2).

Spar sell straightforward wines from Italy. Their white and red Lambrusco are justly popular.

Co-Op offer Lambrusco (£−2).

Marks & Spencer have an excellent Frascati (£2−2.50) and one of the best Lambruscos, red and white, (£−2).

Safeway have a good selection of Italian wines. Their Chianti Ruffino (red) Aziano '83 (£2.50−3), Orvieto Classico '84 (£2.50−3), Marsala (£2.50−3) and Fontana Candida Frascati (£2.50−3) are all excellent.

Asda sell Lambrusco (£−2) and Lago di Caldaro (£2−2.50).

Tanners sell Pinot Grigio '84 (£3+) from the South Tyrol.

And **Majestic Wine Warehouses** sell the lovely, still, sweet Moscato d'Asti (£2.50−3). Try their Chardonnay Tiefenbonner '84 (£3+).

Le Riche's sell a fine Merlot Sironi (£2.50−3 for 2 litres).

Tates sell a lot of their Lambrusco (£−2).

Peter Dominic's Pedrotti Lambrusco (red and white) and their Soave Villa Belvedere are both (£−2).

Wm Low find that their white Lambrusco now outsells the red (£−2) and that their 1½ litre bottles of Soave and Valpolicella sell on their excellent quality/value.

Agnew's white Lambrusco (£−2) and a fine Pinot Grigio (£2.50−3) from the Veneto are well worth a try.

Walter Willson sell a Valpolicella Ambra for (£2−2.50).

Lo-Cost sell a good Chianti (£−2).

Morris's Wine Stores Chianti, Rufina 'Remole' Frescobaldi, is a winner (£3+).

The Victoria Wine Company find that the Piemontello (£2−2.50) sells like mad.

Bottoms Up sell Bacchus Frascati (£2−2.50) from their sizable collection of Italian wines. Their good Lambrusco is (£−2).

Airey's Wine Stores best-sellers are their white and red Lambrusco (£−2).

Barrett – always a place for a bargain – sometimes sell Chianti Classico (£−2) and Bacchus Frascati (£−2).

Drew and **Cellar 5**'s most popular red wine is Lambrusco (£−2). But their red Capricci (£−2), from Bolzano in Alto Adige, is a great success story for customer and merchant alike.

Augustus Barnett, offer a good Lambrusco (£−2).

AUSTRIA

Austria is one of those European countries that have wine-making traditions stretching back to hundreds of years BC.

Although a huge quantity of wine is produced there, not a great deal of it reaches our supermarket shelves. It did in days past, when much of the German Liebfraumilch mix was of Austrian origin. And the Germans still use a lot of it for 'Euroblending' purposes.

Generally speaking, the wine is of a medium-dry style, the best coming from the Wachau region.

Controls over quality are sometimes lax in that country.

AUSTRIAN WINE SELECTION

Schluck is probably the best-known Austrian wine to be seen in supermarkets.

And if you think that after a scandal is a good and safe time to buy, then **Tanners** offer six examples (£2–2.50 upwards).

THE BALKANS

It's almost as if there was a wine-pipe running between our supermarkets and the Balkans – that area of Eastern Europe situated in the peninsula bordered by the Black, Aegean and Adriatic seas. And why not? These countries are going into the wine business in a big way to gain hard currency.

Sometimes you would think that they have some way to go. But, generally speaking, their wines are splendid value and well above average in quality. We shall see and taste more and more of them.

HUNGARY

Hungary has a fine and ancient tradition as a winemaking country land and now produces Olasz Riesling, Bulls Blood and Tokay.

One white wine to look out for, too, is Tramini. With its slight Muscat flavour (and low price), it makes a fine aperitif drink. Serve it cold. But remember that many of these wines are high in alcohol. So consider adopting the Hungarian's practice of adding soda water to them.

Tokay is a most royal and ancient wine that is full, heavy and oxidized. Some of the grape juice added to this wine comes from overripe bunches. This sweetens and strengthens it. Usually found in half litre bottles, the more of this concentrate added, the sweeter will be the wine. Six units is maximum (but rare). You will see the number added written on the label.

HUNGARIAN WINE SELECTION

Safeway have a very good selection of Hungarian wines. Try their Tramini as a white wine with taste, character – and strength (£–2). Their Hungarian Merlot is colourful, soft and easy (£–2).

Bottoms Up have a well-selected list which includes Tokay, the white Somlo Furmint (£2–2.50) and red Sopron Nagyburgundi (£2–2.50).

Waitrose sell a Hungarian Red (£2.50–3 a litre).

Grandways sell Bulls Blood (£–2) (one of the cheapest).

Agnews, Augustus Barnett, Blayney Wines, Dickens Wine House, Kwik-Save and **Foodrite** all sell Bulls Blood in the (£2–2.50) range.

Carrefour offer Cabernet Sauvignon (£–2).

Eldridge Pope sell Bulls Blood (£2.50–3) and Tokay.

Gough Brothers stock Cabernet Sauvignon (£–2), Pinot Noir (£–2) and Bulls Blood (£2–2.50).

Lay & Wheeler sell Tokay.

Sainsbury's offer Olasz Riesling in the three litre box.

Oddbins sell the Cabernet Sauvignon (£–2), Pinot Noir (£–2) and Bulls Blood (£2–2.50).

Peter Dominic offer Cloberg (£2–2.50) and Bulls Blood (£2.50–3).

BULGARIA

Bulgaria is a country where wine traditions stem from classic Greece and before. But it is a far cry from those ancients, crushing grapes between stones, to the modern helicopter, spraying rows of vines that stretch for as far as the eye can see. And if the Bulgars carry on at the rate they're going, we shall see even more of their low-priced, red Cabernet Sauvignons and white Chardonnays on the shelves.

Should you see either of the reds, Asenovgrad Mavrud or Sakar Mountain Cabernet, snap up a bottle or two to try. They have real class – and will still be inexpensive for what they are.

Other names to watch out for are Melnik and Gumza.

Long may the Balkans supply us with a real alternative to our – often price-escalating – regular sources. Supermarket buyers know value when they see it. The Bulgarians are supplying the goods.

BULGARIAN WINE SELECTION

Most High Street outlets now sell Bulgarian wine of one sort or another. All are in the 'above average' category. They are good value wines, too.

Majestic Wine Warehouses are strong in the field. They stock Sakar Mountain and Mavrud, both (£2.50–3), Merlot (£–2), Cabernet Sauvignon and a Red (both £–2). Their white Chardonnay (£–2) is excellent value.

Peter Dominic sell a Mavrud (£2.50–3), Merlot (£–2), a Cabernet Sauvignon (£–2) and a Chardonnay (£–2).

Cullens find their Cabernet Sauvignon (£2–2.50) to be a 'best-seller'.

Agnews sell a Cabernet Sauvignon (£–2) and a Pinot Chardonnay (£–2).

Tanners sell a fine Riesling (£–2), a Cabernet Sauvignon (£–2) and Sakar Mountain Cabernet (£3+).

Bottoms Up offer the red Merlot (£–2) and white Chardonnay (£–2) as well as Sakar Mountain Cabernet '76 & '78.

Asda sell Bulgarian white and red (£–2).

Blayney Wines offer Cabernet Sauvignon '81, a Chardonnay and a Riesling (all £2–2.50).

Carrefour sell a Chardonnay and a Riesling (£–2).

Davisons hold the Riesling, the Cabernet Sauvignon and the Chardonnay (all £2–2.50).

Lay & Wheeler offer their Balkan Selection (£–2), Pinot Chardonnay and Cabernet Sauvignon (£–2).

Dolamore not only offer Sakar Mountain (£2–2.50) but Mavrud, too (£2–2.50) – beside an excellent range (all £–2).

Fullers are very enthusiastic about their Cabernet Sauvignon (£2–2.50) and Mountain Cabernet (£3+).

Gough Brothers sell Cabernet Sauvignon (£–2), Riesling (£–2), Mehana (£–2) and Italianski Riesling (£2–2.50).

Morris's Wine Stores sell a Riesling (£2–2.50). A Cabernet Sauvignon (£2–2.50) and a Chardonnay (£2–2.50).

Oddbins offer Mehana (£–2), **Tesco**, Welsch Riesling (£–2) and **Threshers**, Balkan Cellar (£–2).

Waitrose sell Bulgarian Red (£–2) and Cabernet Sauvignon (£–2).

So you see, the range is fairly limited, but the availability enormous.

ROMANIA

The Romanians seem slow to push their wines onto our supermarket shelves. If the red flow from Count Dracula's land should put you off, there is always romantic Moldavia to put you on.

Among the wines I have tried are a splendid Merlot (so look out for one of those) and others, especially the reds, that have a sweet, overcooked taste so loved by the inhabitants of the Balkans and U.S.S.R.

I think we shall see more of the red and white wines from Romania.

ROMANIAN WINE SELECTION

These wines tend to find their way to specialist wine shops rather than to supermarkets.

However, **Waitrose** have an excellent, white Riesling de Banat (£−2).

Walter Willson offer a Romanian Cabernet Sauvignon (£2−2.50).

Wilsons Wines offer Riesling de Banat (£−2), Bucium Cabernet Sauvignon (£−2) and a most interesting Gewurtztraminer (late picked and very sweet) (£2−2.50).

Leo's offer a Pinot Noir '81 (£−2) and a Riesling '83 (£−2).

YUGOSLAVIA

If many unknown varieties of wine are drunk on the spot by holiday-makers in Yugoslavia, it is to Lutomer and Laski Riesling that they return on reaching home. These are pleasant, straightforward wines in the popular taste. And they must be consumed in enormous quantity, for Yugoslavia enjoys fifth place as wine exporter to this country.

Their Gewurtztraminer is seen here, too. But do not confuse this wine with that from Alsace. It is, however, scentily light and pleasant – well worth a try.

Of the reds, expect more from Merlot than from Cabernet Sauvignon.

YUGOSLAVIAN WINE SELECTION

Many supermarkets and wine stores, like **Safeway, Grandways, Tesco, Waitrose, Gateway, Saverite** and **Agnews** (who also sell Silvainia, Tiger Milk, Pinot Noir and Luternes) offer Lutomer Laski Riesling at (about £2). It is a best-seller with **Walter Willson, Thomas Patterson** and **WM Low**. **Peatling & Cawdron** specialize in this wine. And **VG** have a good selection (£-2).

Some others who sell the same wine at roughly the same price, are **Blayney Wines, Dickens Wine House, Foodrite, Townend, Presto, Sainsbury's, Shoppers Paradise** and **Spar**.

Bottoms Up offer Cloberg and Lutomer Laski Riesling (£-2).

Davisons sell Riesberg Laski Riesling and Tiger Milk (both £2-2.50).

Gough Brothers offer Cloberg Laski Riesling (£-2) and Gewurtztraminer (£2-2.50).

Littlewoods sell Modri Burgundec Pinot Noir (£-2).

Peter Dominic offer Cloberg (£-2), Lutomer (£2-2.50), Gewurtztraminer (£2-2.50) and Tiger Milk (£2-2.50).

Threshers sell their Cloberg Laski Riesling and Lutomer Laski Riesling at (£2-2.50).

And **The Victoria Wine Company** offer a Red and Laski Riesling (both at £-2).

So here again is a seemingly limitless flow of a limited range.

AROUND THE MEDITERRANEAN

Few wines reach us from Islamic Turkey – though perfectly good examples are made in their country and could appear on our shelves.

The resinous Retsina is sometimes seen alongside bottles of presentable white wines from Greece. The better wines are hard to find. Sweet Samos wines have been popular for years.

And from Cyprus come straightforward, sunny wines that are all worth a try – the reds, especially, with kebabs. And their sherry, too, is very popular.

Château Musar, from Lebanon, is a source of fine wine – though not cheap.

Israeli wines, too, are beginning to find their way onto our supermarket shelves. Some reasonably priced Cabernet Sauvignons make excellent alternatives to wines made with the same grape from the Balkans.

Moroccan red wines have lovely colour and taste. Try one if possible.

Algeria, before the French left, supplied us students with fine, strong, no-nonsense plonk. They could do so again. And I am sure that the wine is still of the same 'tough and sunny' order.

These lesser-known wines have to compete for shelf space with many more profitable, fast-selling wines, so they seldom get a look-in. The best way to find a selection from which to choose, would be to seek out imaginative merchants in London's Soho district. Del Monico, in Old Compton Street, should be your first call. You would find four Israeli wines there (£2.50–3) and eight Greek and Cypriot wines for (£–2) upwards. They also stock Château Musar from the Lebanon and Sidi Brahim from Algeria (£2–2.50).

And almost included in this Mediterranean area (if we slip up through the Bosporus to the Black Sea) are the wines of Russia's Crimea. The sweeter edition of Crimean Red goes to Germany, but a dry one is exported to us (£2.50–3). Fruity and full, it is obtainable from the Russian Shop in High Holborn, London.

MEDITERRANEAN WINES SELECTION

CYPRUS

From Cyprus comes Emva Cream sherry (generally £2–2.50). And it finds its way into so many of our High Street outlets, that to list them would be to make a smaller version of our Liebfraumilch collection.

Threshers market their own-brand of Cyprus sherry (£2.50–3).

Davisons sell Red Seal sherry from the same country (£2.50–3).

And the **Co-Op** sell Sodap (£2–2.50).

Quik-Save offer Mosaic Cream (£2–2.50) and **Townend**, Lara (£2–2.50).

Agnews sell Blond Lady (£2–2.50) (a white wine) and Olympus Red (£–2). **Foodrite** offer Mosaic sherry (£2–2.50).

And those litres of sweetish, white Hirondelle come from Cyprus, too.

GREECE

From Greece, **Agnews** sell Retsina (£2.50–3) and Domestica wine (£2.50–3). **Morris's Wine Stores** sell the same, as do **Peter Dominic**.

Waitrose offer a red in Apollo Courtakis (£–2) and Corinth Retsina (£2–2.50).

Oddbins Retsina (£2–2.50) comes from Samos.

Sainsbury's offer a Retsina at (£–2).

Bottoms Up sell Domestica in all colours (£2–2.50) and Danielis red (£2–2.50).

LEBANON

Lebanon is known in the wine world for its Château Musar (£3+). It is obtainable at **Fullers, Tanners, Lay & Wheeler, Peter Dominic, Unwins, Waitrose** and **Bottoms Up**.

ISRAEL

Gough Brothers offer the Israeli wine Palwin No. 10 (£3+).

Tesco sell their Cabernet Sauvignon (£2–2.50), and a fresh young red called Ein Gedi (£–2).

And **Safeway** offer the Israeli Carmel Cabernet Sauvignon '83 (£2–2.50).

ALGERIA

Peter Dominic sell the Algerian Red Infuriator (£2–2.50).

MOROCCO

A Moroccan wine, called Tarik '81 (£2–2.50) is obtainable from **Oddbins**.

SOUTH AFRICA

The South Africans can make superb wine. But, as a South African dealer told me: 'They suffer from sales resistance.'

The Pinotage grape produces excellent, full, winter, red wines, as does the Cabernet Sauvignon. The Chenin Blanc in that country makes wine in a huge range of styles – and most of them are superior.

There wine producers may choose to have their wines 'certified', and most who export do so. These various classifications are indicated on the neck label in the form of coloured stripes.

One Blue band (Origin) means that 100 percent of the wine in the bottle comes from the named district on the label.

One Red band (Vintage) indicates that at least 75 percent of the wine inside is from the harvest year stated.

The Green one means that a minimum percentage of the grape variety indicated is included, and that the wine has the style of that variety.

The 'full house' of the above Blue, Red and Green bands combines their separate meanings with the guarantee that the wine is made from grapes grown on one specific estate, but that it may have been bottled elsewhere.

Blue, Red and Green on a Gold background combines all the above and, in addition, shows that the wine has been assessed as a high quality South African wine.

SOUTH AFRICAN WINE SELECTION

The quality of K.W.V. wines is almost invariably good – as are most South African wines.

Booths sell K.W.V. Cape Nouveau (£2–2.50).

The Victoria Wine Company offer the red Stellenberg Roodekeur (£2–2.50) and Chenin Blanc (£–2).

Davisons sell the K.W.V. range and those from Bertrams.

Dickens Wine House stock their own Chenin Blanc (£2.50–3), Pinotage and Cabernet Sauvignon (£3+).

Fullers offer the K.W.V. wines, as do **Unwins** and **Gough Brothers**.

Tanners sell the wines of K.W.V., Nederberg, Durbanville Estate, Stellenbosch Estate and Groot Constantina (£3+).

Peter Dominic offer the K.W.V. range (£2.50–3).

Threshers stock K.W.V. Rooderberg (£2.50–3) and Chenin Blanc '82 (£2.50–3). They also have Pinotage (£2.50–3).

Morris's Wine Stores offer the K.W.V. range and South African sherries.

Dolamore have an extensive range of South African wines.

Waitrose offer the Culomborg Pinotage '83 (£–2) and Colombar '83 or '84 (£2.50–3). They also have the K.W.V. Chenin Blanc (£2–2.50) and several South African sherries. All these are very good value.

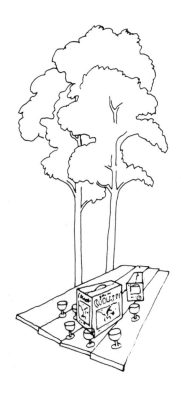

AUSTRALIA

I once wrote that, as far as wine is concerned, Australia would be the next bonanza land. I still believe it.

How is it that with its extremes of climate, Australia can produce wines to compete with, if not surpass, those from the rest of the world? I believe it is the native's sheer inventiveness, brought on by indigenous feelings of 'get stuffed the rest of the globe, we're doing it *our* way', that does the trick. It is with this approach and with dedicated attention – not to mention pockets of ideal climate and soil – that has produced winemakers of international stature.

Australians have used even the most modest of European vine varieties to make superb wine.

Two reds stand out. They are Shiraz (Syrah) and Cabernet Sauvignon. And the blend of the two is a winner.

Of the white varieties used, look out for Chardonnay, Rhein Riesling, Sauvignon Blanc, Marsanne, Chenin Blanc and Grenache.

The names of wine areas, that you will see printed on the label, are indications of quality. Some of the outstanding ones are Barossa and Coonawarra from South Australia, Swan River, Margaret River and Mount Barker from Western Australia, the Hunter Valley in New South Wales and the up and coming Tasmania.

Among the producers names to look for are Penfolds, Lindemans, Rosemount Estate, Wolf Blass, McWilliams, Brown Brothers, Berri Estates, Orlando, Seppelt, Houghton, Wynns and Mitchell.

AUSTRALIAN WINE SELECTION (£3+)

Majestic Wine Warehouses, Cullens, The Victoria Wine Company, Bordeaux Direct, Waitrose, Sainsbury's, Oddbins, Bottoms Up and **Threshers** all stock fine Australian wines.

Why not start out with a modestly priced one in Houghton Supreme from **Waitrose**? Then go on to a Rosemount Chardonnay from **Peter Dominic** (and elsewhere). A splendid red Cabernet Sauvignon from the same vineyard will cost you about the same from **The Victoria Wine Company** – which, like the others, is over our £3 cut-off mark. **Eldridge Pope**'s Seppelt Chardonnay '83 is a beauty.

But although most of these Australian wines are expensive, they are still excellent value when considering their overall, high quality.

UK SHOPS AND AUSTRALIAN SUPPLIERS

Here are the names of some shops and their suppliers in Australia:

Tanners: Stanley Watervale, Leasingham, Wynns, Hill-Smith, Hardy's and Tisdall.

Dolamore: Penfolds.

Eldridge Pope: Seppelt and Brown Bros.

Waitrose: Houghton and Berri Estates.

Fullers: Berri Estate and Rosemount Estate.

Dickens Wine House: Brown Bros.

Townend: Hill-Smith.
Peter Dominic: Tollana and Rosemount Estate.
Unwins: Rosemount Estate.
Tesco: Wynns, Berri Estates and Renmano Wines.
Majestic Wine Warehouses: Hardy's, Brown Bros. and Rosemount Estate.
Gough Brothers: Rosemount Estate.
Bottoms Up: Berri Estates and Rosemount Estate.
Booths: Brown Bros. and Rosemount Estate.

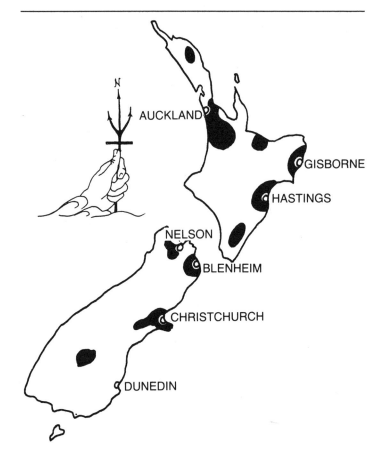

NEW ZEALAND

The maritime climate of New Zealand would seem to favour, if anything, the production of white wine. It does. And in considering their wines it is best to concentrate on their 'delicacy'.

Let's look at some whites first.

Cooks Chenin Blanc can be as good a wine made from this grape variety as you will taste. The same firm produces a fine Gewurtztraminer, too.

And Montana Chardonnay may well surpass those wines made from this grape variety from many more famous lands.

Wines made from the Sauvignon Blanc are exceeding the quality of those made from this grape in the Loire. Even the humble Muller Thurgau can be turned into a special wine by New Zealand winemakers. These varieties have emigrated with great success to this part of the Antipodes.

The climate would not seem to favour the production of red wine. But sometimes a startlingly good one will appear.

Cooks Hawkes Bay Cabernet Sauvignon can be good.

And a South African red grape does well in their soil, so Montana's Pinotage is worth a try.

NEW ZEALAND WINES SELECTION

Bottoms Up offer Cooks New Zealand Red (£2.50–3) and Chenin Blanc (£3+).

Oddbins have the Montana Sauvignon Blanc '82 and Chardonnay '82 (£3+).

Peter Dominic offer Cooks White and Red (£2.50–3), the Chenin Blanc and Muller Thurgau (£3+).

And **Townend** stock Cooks New Zealand Chenin Blanc (£2.50–3) and Cooks Sauvignon (£3+).

Carrefour offer Cooks N.Z. Red (£2–2.50) and **Fullers**, Cooks Red and White (£2.50–3).

Waitrose, too, have the White and Red (£2.50–3) and a Cabernet Sauvignon '83 (£3+).

Lay & Wheeler sell Cooks Muller Thurgau (£2.50–3) and their Gewurtztraminer (£3+).

Tanners have an extensive list of Montana wines (£3+).

U.S.A.

With over-production of wine in the United States, it is surprising that we do not see more of this surplus on our supermarket shelves.

Anyone familiar with the custom of quaffing down vast goblets of 'Chablis' on their own home ground, will have been seduced by the charms of its style and of its red fellows.

The closest we get to it here is wine in those most-marketed carafes (often, sadly, down to 70 cl, when only the correct 75 cl would have been permissible in the country of its origin). This white wine is sold as 'white' or 'dry white'. The white is the one to aim for. It has that degree of sweetness that enhances its fruitiness. These wines should be drunk up quickly. Their delicacy of flavour can evaporate in a day or two.

The red carafe is a fine, if heady, all-round wine.

Other bottles appear from time to time. And sometimes they are real bargains.

The Cabernet Sauvignon grape does well in the New World by producing a dense, full wine. But, when mass-produced, it is without the finesse of wines made from this grape, elsewhere. But what it loses in nuances, it gains in power.

The finest Californian wines compare with any – anywhere. But the price of these exclude them from our supermarket shelves.

Take it that American wines are marketed to be drunk right away. So there's little point in 'giving them time'.

U.S.A. WINE SELECTION

The ubiquitous Paul Masson Carafes are to be seen on so many shelves that I will not list them. They come as Medium Dry White, Dry White, Red and Rosé. The size was originally of a litre capacity, but they are now obtainable in the 70 cl quantity (£2.50–3).

Lay & Wheeler have a very good list of Californian wines, with examples from Round Hill, Stags Leap, Mondavi, Jordan, Trefethen, Conn Creek, Jordan Vineyards and St. Clement

(£3+). The price of any one of these beauties is, of course, somewhat above our cut-off mark.

Eldridge Pope is another wine merchant with such a fine list. **Tanners** is another where they add the wines of Ridge, Trefethen, Joseph Phelps and Heitz (£3+).

Waitrose have Fetzer Zinfandel '80 and North Coast Cellars Chenin Blanc (£3+).

Fullers have Californian reds and whites (£2.50–3).

Sainsbury's sell Californian White and Red (£2–2.50) with Sainsbury's Zinfandel (£3+).

The Victoria Wine Company sell the robust Franzia (£3+).

Bottoms Up offer Paul Masson's Cabernet Sauvignon and Chardonnay, as do **Carrefour** (£3+).

Asda stock Paul Masson Chardonnay and Zinfandel (£3+).

Agnews sell Mountain Red and White (£2.50–3).

Majestic Wine Warehouses offer not only Geoffrey Roberts Reserve Red and White (£2.50–3) but wines from Mondavi, Stags Leap and Heitz as well (£3+).

And we mustn't forget the de-alcoholized Paul Masson Light White (£–2) from **Sainsbury's**.

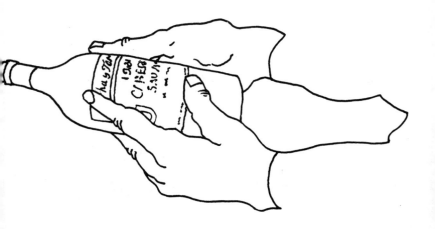

SOUTH AMERICA

A vast amount of wine is made in South America. But, diplomatic relations permitting, only a few of their wines appear on our supermarket shelves. It is mainly Chilean wine that finds its way to our shores at present, and their Cabernet Sauvignon may surprise you with its class.

SOUTH AMERICAN WINE SELECTION

Dickens Wine House offer three Chilean wines in Concha y Toro, Cabernet Sauvignon with Cousino-Macul's Chardonnay and Cabernet Sauvignon (£3+).

    Tanners sell another Chilean Cabernet Sauvignon in Vina Linderos '82 (£3+).

    Booths offer an upper-class Chilean called Antiguas Reservas Cousino-Macul '77 (£3+).

    Peatling & Cawdron stock a good Chilean Cabernet from Miguel Torres (£3+).

    Waitrose sell Concha y Toro Cabernet Sauvignon '82 (£2.50–3) – the only one I have found below our cut-off mark.

    Oddbins offer the same (1980).

    Davisons sell another Cabernet Sauvignon, called Vina Linderos '82 (£3+).

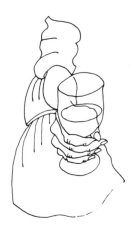

ENGLISH WINE

One thing is for sure, real English white wine ('British Wine' is not made from English grapes), when fermented out to its dry state, has real style. If drunk young, it is fresh, clean and delightful. I have not tasted a great one.

When vinifiers turn this wine into a sweet or sweetish edition – to catch a 'popular' market – they ape the Germans and, I believe, fail in their attempts. Then it is better to buy German wine, well made, and at far less cost.

And here's the rub. English wine is not only subjected to high taxation but has – and will have for some time yet – a novelty value. Both of these aspects tend to keep the price of a bottle above its true worth.

Try our very own wine, please. But don't pay too much for it. Prices are coming down to more realistic levels. Sense prevails.

ENGLISH WINE SELECTION

The cheapest I have found, so far, is **Safeway**'s Lamberhurst (£2–2.50).

Tanners sell Three Choirs Muller Thurgau/Reichensteiner '83, Newhall's Huxelrebe '82 and '83, and Broadfield Court Seyve-Villard and Adgestone wine (all £3+). That's a good selection.

Foodrite sell Lamberhurst, **Eldridge Pope**, Wraxall and Pilton Manor, and **Dickens Wine House**, Adgestone Vineyards (all £3+).

Waitrose sell Carr Taylor's Reichensteiner '83 and '84 (£2.50–3) and Fonthill (£3+). They also have Lymington Vineyards (£3+).

Davisons offer Lamberhurst Priory Muller Thurgau '83 (£3+).

British Home Stores stock English Table '83 (£3+).

Townend sell Lamberhurst (£2.50–3).

Oddbins have Lamberhurst Reichensteiner '83 (£3+).

Peter Dominic sell Lamberhurst Priory Muller Thurgau (£2.50–3) and Carr Taylor Gutenborner (£3+).

Unwins sell Lamberhurst '84 (£2.50–3), and **Tesco** sell a reasonably priced one in Saint Edmund (£2–2.50).

Bottoms Up have a good collection in Three Choirs '82 and '83 (£2.50–3), Carr Taylor Gutenborner '82 (£2.50–3), besides wine from Lamberhurst and Ditchling Vineyards (£3+).

Majestic Wine Warehouses offer Bruisyard St. Peter '83 (£2.50–3) and Adgestone '82 (£3+).

Sainsbury's stock Biddenden Ortega '83 (£3+).

Sherston offer Bruisyard St. Peter Muller Thurgau '83, Wraxall Muller Thurgau '83 and Sherston Earl '84 (all £3+).

So you see, there are quite a few about – and I'm sure there will be more.

BRITISH WINE

British wines enjoy tremendous sales in this country. They are 'British' because they are processed here. The basic, grape juice concentrate from which they are made comes from abroad.

One of the most popular, Country Manor, is not connected with the grape at all. It is perry – made from pears. And as these pears are English, it really is British.

Rougemont Castle, Concorde, Country Carafe and Chambard are others based on the grape. Sold in bottle or box as red, white, dry white and rosé, they are to be found on many supermarket shelves.

My sentiments about them are much the same as for Euroblends – being that they have a real place in catering for those who cannot afford more. But in this case, the very concentrating of grape juice, presumably by heat, does destroy some properties of the grape that Euroblends maintain. There seems to be less destruction in the case of sherries.

It is my feeling that, for a few pence more per bottle, there is an attractive, seductive and beautiful world of wine, waiting to be embraced.

BRITISH WINE SELECTION

To make a list of the outlets for British wines and sherries would, I think, be as long, if not longer, than that for Liebfraumilch. But here are some popular brands – and their prices are always very reasonable.

Wines: Country Manor, Concorde, Chambard, Rougemont Castle, Country Carafe, Belgrove Carafe.

Sherries: QC range, Old England, Spring Grove, Presto British, Sainsbury's British, VP range, Hudson & Cooper, Gold Dust, Prestige British Sherry, Anglia British Sherry, Waitrose British Sherry, Old Manor House, B.V.P.

Ports: British Ruby, British Rich Ruby, Old Manor House.

Then there are those stalwarts in Crabbies and Stones Ginger Wine. And sensible people will warm themselves in the wintertime by mixing either of these with any kind of whisky – in proportions to suit.

VINTAGE DATES

Do not concern yourself too much with vintage dates. Supermarkets will seldom sell a dud wine – even from a bad year. Anyway, good wines – or adequate wines – are always made in 'off' years, and they will be good value.

It is true that a wine from a recognized 'good' vintage will lie more happily in the cellar for longer. But these vintages are not always immediately apparent – even to the 'experts'. Anyway, a little time after the harvest is necessary before a balanced judgement can be made.

The red Bordeaux from the years of '82 and '83 stand out. The whites from that area did well in '81 and '83. The '84s in general were better than anticipated, and the '85s are generally splendid.

Do not worry about Champagne vintage dates.

Red and white Burgundies did well in '82 and '83. They are the ones to aim for. The '85s look very good.

The Loires of '82 shine out – as they did in Alsace. And '85s are good.

As in Burgundy, the northern Rhône wines (Hermitage, Crozes-Hermitage and St. Joseph, etc.) of '83 are extremely fine. The 82s are excellent, too. '85s are great.

In the southern Rhône (Châteauneuf du Pape and the Côtes du Rhône, etc.), the recent years have been of much the same quality. 85s are splendid.

Italian wines, generally, did well in '83, but even better in '82. (Barolo made fine wine from '83 back to '79, Chianti in '82 and '81, Valpolicella in '83 and '82). All offer excellent 1985.

In Rioja the '81s and '82s were well above average in quality. With wines from the rest of Spain, look for those of '81 and '84. The '85 Riojas omen well for the future.

The Vintage Ports of '83, '77, '70, '66 and '63 were all excellent. For the rest of Portugal look out for '82 and '80 especially. '85 could turn out well.

The '84 wines from California were outstanding. – the '85s, too.

In Germany the '83s were superb, closely followed by the '82s. Now we have the '85s to look forward to.

Australia is too large a country and its climates too diverse to be able to generalize on vintages.

South Africa. The 1984s are full and good.

Generally speaking, 1984 was not the bad year that it was made out to be. But prices rose more than they should. The fine '85 wines will often be great. Some, possibly, really great. And prices? They will depend on the good sense of the trade. Lower down the scale of quality, prices are good.

For quality combined with value, those '82s and '83s will be the ones to acquire – for a year or two yet.

If, like most of us, you become a bit flummoxed in a restaurant when confronted with a long wine list, and cannot clamp your eye on a certainty through knowledge, either go for a carafe or bottle of the house red or white, or, an almost better alternative, is to ask the *advice* of the waiter: "With your knowledge and experience, perhaps you would recommend a sound (whatever type you fancy) at a modest price." Then, remembering a few of the dates above could come in handy.

One is either rich, extremely discerning or foolish to order fine wine at a restaurant in France. You will probably be just as happy, if not much happier, swilling down cold Muscadet or Gros Plant for white, and Côtes du Rhône for red. And as you will not be soaked for either – aim for both. Buy fine French wines in England.

CONCLUSION

We in Britain are surely the luckiest wine-consumers in the world. It is true that in most countries of origin, basic wines are cheaper by far. But when it comes to a country for choice and quality, we are unbeatable. And, thanks to our supermarket buyers – and cut-throat competition between them – we are offered a mass of the world's wines at very fair prices.

Should one country become greedy and overcharge for its vinous products, another will very soon take its place. That is where we come in as consumers. To ensure the continuation of good value, we must not adhere to any one country or style of wine. There is plenty of quality about from which to choose. So price, imagination and flexibility must be our watchwords. Trust your own judgement.

CHOOSING WINE FROM SOME MAJOR OUTLETS

The following constitutes a quick reference guide when buying from the plethora of bottles offered by some selected wine stores and supermarkets in the High Street.

A few bottles listed here are not mentioned in the text. They are good value wines, added to give you a wider choice when selecting from the shelves.

All the information is correct at time of going to press; but remember that the best wines sell fastest, so if you should find some wines are no longer available, buy your copy of this guide earlier next year to benefit from the best buys.

A note to tell me of any wines that are failing in quality, or others that should be mentioned, will be much appreciated (remembering that it is good CHEAP ones that we are really after). Although I cannot promise to reply, I will most certainly take note. And let us hope that such correspondence will be to our mutual satisfaction. Thank you.

AGNEWS

WHITES

Sortima Tafelwein Euroblend (£−2).
Bulgarian Pinot Chardonnay (£−2).
Lutomer Riesling (£−2). Tiger milk (£−2). Silvania (£−2).
    Luternes (£−2).
Liebfraumilch (£−2).
Lambrusco Bianco (£−2).
Blanc Anjou (£2−2.50). Dry.
Vinho Verde (£2−2.50).
Blond Lady (Cyprus) (£2−2.50).
Deinard Niersteiner Gutes Domtal '82 (£2.50−3).
Pinot Grigio (£2.50−3). Dry.
Retsina (£2.50−3).
Californian Mountain White (£2.50−3).
Sancerre Garennes (£3+). Dry.
Hill-Smith Riesling (£3+).

REDS & ROSÉS

Yugoslavian Pinot Noir (£−2).
Bulgarian Cabernet Sauvignon (£−2).
Greek Olympus (£−2).
Lambrusco Rovervini (£−2).
Bardolino Leonardo (£−2).
Bulls Blood (£2−2.50).
Greek Domestica (£2−2.50).
Côtes du Rhône (£2−2.50).
Californian Mountain Red (£2.50−3).
Crozes-Hermitage (£2.50−3).
Mateus White and Rosé (£2.50−3).
Château la Valade (£3+).

SWEET WINES

Castillo de Liria (£−2).
Binger St. Rochus Auslese (£3+).

SPARKLING WINES

Duc Du Monteronne (£3+).

Moscato Spumante (£3+).
Sparkling Blue Nun (£3+).

SHERRY

QC Cream (£−2). (British).
Old England (£2−2.50). (British).
Croft Original (£3+).

PORT

Taylor's Ruby (£3+).
Cockburn's Special Reserve (£3+).

AIREY'S WINE STORES

WHITES

Liebfraumilch (£−2).
Lambrusco Bianco (£−2).

REDS

Lambrusco Rosso (£−2).
Côtes du Rhône Château Grand Moulas '84 (£2.50−3).

SWEET WINES

Barsac (£3+).

SPARKLING WINES

Rôbe d'Or (£2.50−3).
Baron de Beaupré (£3+).

SHERRY

Don Peppino (£2.50−3).

PORT

Quinta da Noval LB (£3+).

ARTHUR RACKHAM

WHITES

Corbières, Roussillon and Languedoc (£2–2.50). Dry.

REDS

Corbières, Roussillon and Languedoc (£2–2.50).

SPARKLING WINES

They have a wonderful list of Champagnes from which to choose (£3+).

SHERRY

Sandemans (£3+).

PORT

Ferreira LBV '80 (£3+).

ASDA

WHITES

Bulgarian White (£–2).
Don Cortez White (£–2).
Bulgarian Riesling (£–2).
Bereich Berncastle (£–2).
Niersteiner Gutes Domtal (£–2).
Liebfraumilch (£–2).
Lambrusco (£–2).
Domaine de la Jalousie (£2–2.50). Dry.
Domaine Manaut (Alella) (£2.50–3). Dry.
Gatão Vinho Verde (£2.50–3).
Nussdorfer Bischopkreuz '83 (£2.50–3).
Paul Masson Chardonnay (£3+).

REDS

Bulgarian Red (£−2).
Don Cortez (£−2).
Minervois (£−2).
Claret (£−2).
Bergerac (£−2).
Lambrusco (£−2).
Corbières (£−2).
Lago di Caldaro (£2−2.50).
Bulgarian Cabernet Sauvignon (£2−2.50).
Rioja Bodegas Santana (£2.50−3).
Le Piat d'Or (£3+).
Paul Masson Cabernet Sauvignon (£3+).

SWEET WINES

Asda sweet Bordeaux (£−2).
Château Pistolet '83.

SPARKLING WINES

Vin Mousseux (£2.50−3).
Moscato Spumante (£2.50−3).
Schloss Freidenstein (£2.50−3).
Moët & Chandon Champagne (£3+).

SHERRY

Asda Montilla (£−2).
Emva Cream (Cyprus) (£2−2.50).
Asda Sherry (£2−2.50).
Double Century (£2.50−3).
Harvey's Bristol Cream (£3+).

PORT

Croft Distinction (Old Tawny) (£3+).
Cockburn's Fine Old Ruby (£3+).
Dow Late Bottled '79 (£3+).

ASHE & NEPHEW

WHITES

Liebfraumilch (£−2).
Domaine du Tariquet (Gascogne) (£2−2.50). Dry.
Muscadet sur Lie (£2.50−3). Dry.
Marques de Riscal (£3+). Dry.

REDS

Boulevard (£−2).
Buzet (£2−2.50).
Domaine de Eulalie (Minervois) (£2−2.50).
Fitou (£2−2.50).
Marques de Riscal (£3+).

SPARKLING WINES

Moscato Spumante (£2−2.50).
Sparkling Saumur (£3+).

SHERRY

Thresher's (£2.50−3).

PORT

Ferreira Ruby and LB (£3+).

AUGUSTUS BARNETT

WHITES

Liebfraumilch (£−2).
Lambrusco (£−2).
Lechine Vin de Table (£2−2.50). Dry.

REDS

Lambrusco (£−2).

Carousel (£−2).
Bulls Blood (£2−2.50).
Lechine Vin de Table (£2−2.50).
Côtes du Roussillon Villages (£2−2.50).
Rioja Campo Viejo (£2.50−3).
Crozes-Hermitage (£3+).

SPARKLING WINES

Sparkling Donnilla (£−2).
Moscato Spumante Ambra (£2.50−3).

SHERRY

Harvey's, Croft's and Williams & Humbert Dry Sack (£3+).

PORT

Cockburn's and Warre's (£3+).

BEJAM

WHITES

Domkellerstolz Euroblend (£2−2.50).
Dr. Willkomm's litres (£2.50−3) and three litre boxes of Liebfraumilch (£3+).
Dr. Willkomm's three litre boxes of Tafelwein Euroblend (£3+).

BOOTHS

WHITES

Liebfraumilch (£−2).
Nierstein Spiegleberg '83 (£2−2.50).
Selection Auvigue (£2.50−3). Dry.
Rosemount Estate Australian wines (£3+).

REDS

Booths Table Red, Grains des Noirots (£−2).
Vacqueyras '79 (£2.50−3).
Château Smith Haut Lafite, Graves, '76 (£3+).

SWEET WINE

Muscat de Rivesalte, Château de Jau (£3+).

SPARKLING WINE

Booths Cava and Booths Champagne (£3+).

SHERRY

Booths (£2.50−3).

PORT

Booths Ruby and Vintage Character (£3+).

BLAYNEY WINES

WHITES

Deutcher Tafelwein (£−2).
Mosel Tafelwein (£−2).
Liebfraumilch (£−2).
Klosterschoppen Euroblend (£−2).
Bulgarian Chardonnay and Riesling (£−2).

REDS

Bordeaux La Navette (£2−2.50).
Minervois (£2−2.50).
Cabernet Sauvignon (Aude) (£2−2.50).
Côtes du Rhône Domaine de la Patrasse (£3+).
Châteauneuf du Pape La Pontificale (£3+).
Château Rocher Beauregard, Pomerol, '80 (£3+).

SWEET WINE

Premières Côtes de Bordeaux (£2.50–3).

SPARKLING WINES

Moscato Spumante (£2–2.50).
André Gallois (£3+).
Laurent Perrier Champagne (£3+).

SHERRY

James Bell Sherries (£2.50–3).

PORT

Pocas Ruby and Tawny (£3+).

BOTTOMS UP

WHITES

Kurprinz Liebfraumilch (£–2).
Cloberg and Laski Riesling (£–2).
Bulgarian Chardonnay (£–2). Dry.
Lambrusco (£–2).
Orvieto Secco (£2–2.50). Dry.
Frascati Bacchus (£2–2.50). Dry.
Somlo Furmint (£2–2.50).
Gros Plant sur Lie (£2.50–3). Dry.
Several Alsatian wines (£2.50–3).
Bereich Johannisberg Riesling (£2.50–3).
Carr Taylor and Three Choirs, English (£2.50–3).
Sudtiroler Gewurtztraminer (£3+).
Cune Monopole Rioja (£3+). Dry.
Cooks Chenin Blanc (N.Z.) (£3+). Dry.
Lamberhurst and Ditchling (English) (£3+).
Paul Masson Chardonnay (£3+).

REDS

Bulgarian Merlot (£−2).
Lambrusco (£−2).
Beaujolais Nouveau (£−2).
Greek Domestica (£2−2.50) and Daniellis (£3+).
Sopron Nagyburgundi (£2−2.50).
Côtes du Rhône Domaine de la Chartreuse (£2.50−3).
Bulgarian Mavrud (£2.50−3) and Sakar Mountain (£2.50−3).
Cooks New Zealand (£2.50−3).
Berri Estates Cabernet Shiraz (£3+).
Thirty six fine Riojas (£3+).
Senorio de los Llanos Gran Reserva (£3+).
Château Musar (£3+).
Paul Masson Cabernet Sauvignon (£3+).

SWEET WINES

Beaumes de Venise (£3+).
Tokay (£3+).

SPARKLING WINES

Asti Cinzano (£2.50−3).
Castellenblanch Cava (£3+).
Pol Roger Champagne (£3+).
Mumm's Champagne (£3+).

SHERRY

The Dominicus range (£2.50−3).

PORT AND MADEIRA

Graham's Late Bottled Vintage '79 (£3+).
Croft Triple Crown Ruby and Tawny (£3+).
Blandy's range of Madeiras (£3+).

BRITISH HOME STORES

WHITES

Bordeaux Blanc (£2–2.50). Dry.
Liebfraumilch (£2–2.50).
Alsace Edelswicker (£2.50–3). Dry.
Vouvray (£2.50–3).
English Table Wine (£3+).
Alsace Gewurtztraminer (£3+).

REDS AND ROSÉ

French Carafe (£2–2.50).
Rioja (£2.50–3).
Claret (£2.50–3).
Chianti in flask (£2.50–3).
Château Montaud '83 (dry rosé from Provence) (£3+).

SWEET WINES

Premières Côtes de Bordeaux (£2.50–3).
Sauternes (£3+).

SPARKLING WINES

German Sparkling (£2.50–3).
Asti Spumante (£3+).
Champagne (£3+).

SHERRY

British Home Stores Sherry (£3+).

PORT AND MADEIRA

British Home Stores Fine Old Ruby (£3+).
British Home Stores Malmsey Madeira (Cossart Gordon)
 (£3+).

BUDGEN

WHITES

Liebfraumilch (£−2).
Niersteiner Gutes Domtal (£−2).
Lambrusco (£−2).
Piemontello (−2).
Corbières Blanc de Blancs '84 (£−2).
Spanish White (£−2).
Listel (£2−2.50).

REDS

Lambrusco (£−2).
Corbières (£−2).
Vin de Pays de l'Aude (£−2).
Fitou (£2−2.50).
Claret (£2−2.50).
Côtes du Rhône (£2−2.50).
Beaujolais (£2.50−3).

SPARKLING WINES

Moscato Spumante (£2−2.50).
Champagne Massé (£3+).
Moët & Chandon Champagne (£3+).

SHERRY

Budgen's British (£−2).
Emva (Cyprus) (£2.50−3).
Spanish (£2.50−3).
Gonzales Byass La Concha (£2.50−3).

PORT

Seagrams Founders Reserve (£3+).
Taylor's Late Bottled Vintage (£3+).
Croft Triple Crown (£3+).

CARREFOUR

WHITES

Liebfraumilch (£−2).
Bulgarian Chardonnay (£−2). Dry.
Bulgarian Riesling (£−2).
Blanc de Blancs Charentais (£−2). Dry.
Hungarian Chardonnay (£−2). Dry.
Hallgarten's '84 Neirsteiner Gutes Domtal (£2−2.50).
Saumur Blanc (£2−2.50).
Vina Esmeralda (£2.50−3). Dry.
Paul Masson Chardonnay (£3+).

REDS

Hungarian Cabernet Sauvignon (£−2).
Chinon '84 (£2−2.50).
French litres of Vin de Table (£2−2.50 a litre).
Cooks New Zealand Red (£2−2.50).
Bergerac (£2−2.50).
Buzet (£2.50−3).
Tres Torres (£2.50−3).
Château Tour Prignac (£2.50−3).
Crozes-Hermitage (£2.50−3).
Château Balac '81 (£3+).
Berri Estates Cabernet Shiraz (£3+).
Paternina '76 Rioja (£3+).
Paul Masson Cabernet Sauvignon (£3+).

SWEET WINES

Monbazillac (£2−2.50).
Barsac (£3+)
Sauternes (£3+).
Beaumes de Venise (£3+).

SPARKLING WINES

String of Pearls (Cider) (£−2).
Moscato Ambra (£2−2.50).
Monistrol Cava (£3+).
Brut de Listel (£3+).
Moët & Chandon Champagne (£3+).

SHERRY

Old England (British) (£−2).
Emva Cream (Cyprus) (£2−2.50).
Croft Original (£3+).

PORT

Noval L.B. (£3+).
Croft Triple Crown (£3+).
Sandeman Founders Reserve (£3+).

CO-OP

WHITES

Liebfraumilch (£−2).
Lambrusco (£−2).
Romanian Riesling '83 (£−2) (at **Leo's**).
Lohengrin Bereich Nierstein (£2−2.50).
Black Tower (£2.50−3).

REDS

Romanian Pinot Noir '81 (£−2) (at **Leo's**).
Côtes du Rhône (£−2).
Corrida (£−2).
Lambrusco (£−2).
Beaujolais (£2−2.50).

SPARKLING WINES

Ponte Spumante (£2.50–3).
Veuve du Vernay (£3+).

SHERRY

Old England (British) (£–2).
Sodap (Cyprus) (£2.50–3).
Croft Original (£3+).

PORT

Cassons Ruby (£3+).
Cockburn's Fine Old Ruby (£3+).

CULLENS

WHITES

Bulgarian Mehana (£–2).
Liebfraumilch (£2–2.50).
House Cachet (£2–2.50).
Muscadet (£2–2.50).
Hock and Mosel Tafelwein (£2.50–3).

REDS

Bulgarian Mehana (£–2).
Bulgarian Cabernet Sauvignon (£2–2.50).
House Cachet (£2–2.50).
Jaboulet Isnard St. Joseph (£3+).
Louis Jadot Burgundies (£3+).

SWEET WINES

Bulgarian sweet (£–2).
Château Russec (£3+).

SPARKLING WINES
Neufchatel Brut, Sec and Demi-sec (£2.50–3).

SHERRY
Own Label Cullens (£3+).

PORT
Cockburn's, Dow's and Taylor's LBV (£3+).

DAVISONS

WHITES
Pampette (£–2). Dry.
Liebfraumilch (£2–2.50).
Riesberg Lutomer Riesling and Tiger Milk (£2–2.50).
Bulgarian Riesling and Chardonnay (£2–2.50). Dry.
Hugel Alsace wines (£3+).
Lamberhurst Priory (English) (£3+).

REDS
Pampette (£–2).
Côtes du Rhône (£2–2.50).
Bordeaux Rouge (£2.50–3).
Côtes du Beaune Villages '84 (£2.50–3).
Mâcon Rouge (£2.50–3).
Crozes-Hermitage '82 Caves des Clairmonts (£3+).
Chilean Cabernet Sauvignon Vina Linderos '82 (£3+).
The Beaujolais of Georges Duboeuf (£3+).

SWEET WINE
Beaumes de Venise (£3+).

SPARKLING WINES

Moscato Spumante (£2.50−3).
Asti Spumante Martini (£3+).

SHERRY

Don Avides (£2.50−3).

PORT AND MADEIRA

Smith Woodhouse Ruby (£3+).
Duke of Clarence Malmsey (£3+).

DEL MONICO

WHITES

Blanc de Blancs (£−2). Dry.
Finatello Trebiano (£−2). Dry.
Soave (£−2). Dry.
Badascony Szurkebarat (£2−2.50).
Carmel Chenin Blanc (£3+). Dry.

REDS

Hungarian Taban (£−2).
Corsican Domaine de Fontanella (£−2).
Otello (Cyprus) (£2−2.50).
Carmel No. 11 (£2.50−3) (and Kosha wines from other
  countries).

SPARKLING WINES

Duc de Lamart (£2.50−3).
Italvini Brut (£2.50−3).

DICKENS WINE HOUSE

WHITES

Liebfraumilch (£2–2.50).
Europa Euroblend (£–2).
Bernkasteler Kurfurslay (£2–2.50).
Muscadet (£2–2.50). Dry.
Lutomer Laski Riesling (£2–2.50).
South African Chenin Blanc (£2.50–3).
Adgestone (English) (£3+).

REDS AND ROSÉ

Rosé d'Anjou (£2–2.50).
Vin de Table, Tête de Talbot (£–2).
Vin de Table, Petit Fort (£2–2.50).
Bulgarian Mehana (£–2).
Mâcon (£2.50–3).
Beaujolais Chiroubles (£3+).
Chilean Cousino-Macul's Cabernet Sauvignon (£3+).

SWEET WINE

Graves (£3+).
Sauternes Château Dudon '83 (£3+).

SPARKLING WINES

Duc de Florincourt (£3+).
Sparkling Saumur (£3+).

SHERRY

Jose Cabrera range (£2.50–3).

PORT

Dickens Old Ruby (£3+).
Dickens Vintage Character (£3+).

DOLAMORE

WHITES

Tafelwein Euroblend (£−2).
Blanc de Blancs (£−2). Dry.
Muscadet (£−2). Dry.
College Hock (£2−2.50).

REDS

Bulgarian Mehana (£−2).
Algerian Sidi Brahim (£−2).
Mâcon (£2−2.50).
College Claret (£2−2.50).
Bulgarian Sakar Mountain and Mavrud (£2−2.50).
Bilbainas Pomal Junior Rioja (£2.50−3).

SWEET WINE

Dolamore Sauternes (£3+).
Beaumes de Venise (£3+).

SPARKLING WINE

Club Prestige (£2−2.50).

SHERRY

The College Selection (£2.50−3).

PORT AND MADEIRA

Dolamore's Madeira (£3+).
Fonseca Bin 27 (£3+).

DREW & CELLAR 5

WHITES

Grunnengold Euroblend (£−2).
Lambrusco (£−2).
Soave (£−2). Dry.
Liebfraumilch (£2−2.50).
Piesporter (£2.50−3).
Wiltinger Scharzberg Kabinet (£2.50−3).

REDS

Capricci (Bolzano) (£−2).
Lambrusco (£−2).

SPARKLING WINES

Lanza Moscato (£2.50−3).
René Florancy Champagne (£3+).

SHERRY

Five Cellars brand (£2.50−3).

PORT

Dow's Ruby (£3+).

ELDRIDGE POPE

WHITES

Grand Chevalier Blanc Sec (£2−2.50). Dry.
Cuvée Royale Blanc (£2−2.50). Dry.
Alsace wines of Dopff & Irion and Louis Sipp (£3+).
Seppelt Reserve Bin Chardonnay '83 (£2.50−3).
Wraxall and Pilton Manor English (£3+).

REDS

Grand Chevalier Rouge (£2–2.50).
Cuvée Royale Rouge (£2–2.50).
Prince Louis Claret (£2.50–3).
Fine list of Beaujolais (£3+).

SWEET WINES

Beaumes de Venise (£3+).
Tokay (£3+).

SPARKLING WINES

Veuve Valmante Brut (£3+).
Many Champagnes (£3+).

SHERRY

Chairman's Fino (£3+).

PORT & MADEIRA

Chairman's Port (also in half bottles) (£3+).
Rutherford & Miles Madeiras (£3+).

FINE FARE & CITY GROCERS

WHITES

Spanish Dry White (£–2).
Liebfraumilch (£–2).
Chenin Blanc Jardin de la France (£–2). Dry.
Vinho Verde (£2–2.50).
Piesporter Michelberg (£2.50–3).

REDS

Lambrusco (£−2).
Fine Fare Spanish Red (£−2).
French Red Wine, Vignerons Catalans (£−2).
Rioja Bodegas Franco Espanoles '82 (£2−2.50).
Le Piat d'Or (£2.50−3).
Côtes du Rhône (£2.50−3).
Côtes du Roussillon (£2−2.50).

SWEET WINES

Sweet Bordeaux Blanc (£2−2.50).
Fine Fare Sweet Spanish (£−2).

SPARKLING WINES

Moscato Spumante (Fine Fare) (£2−2.50).
Sparkling Saumur (£3+).

SHERRY

Cream Montilla (£−2).
Emva Cream (Cyprus) (£2−2.50).
Fine Fare Mandola (£2.50−3).

PORT

Fine Fare Ruby (£3+).
Fine Fare Vintage Character (£3+).

FOODRITE

WHITES

Liebfraumilch (£−2).
White Loire, Georges Rousseau (£−2). Dry.
Lutomer Laski Riesling (£−2).
Englehof's Moselblumchen (£2−2.50).
Lamberhurst (English) (£2.50−3).

REDS

Red Loire, Georges Rousseau (£–2).
Bulls Blood (£2–2.50).

SWEET WINES

Coteaux du Layon (£2–2.50).
Monbazillac (£2.50–3).

SPARKLING WINES

Valentin (Loire) (£2.50–3).
Sparkling Saumur (£2.50–3).

SHERRY

Mosaic Cyprus Sherry (£2–2.50).
Wisdom & Warter range (£2.50–3).

PORT

Cockburn's (£3+).

FULLERS AND BUNCHES

WHITES

Vin de Pays Charantais (£–2).
Cépage Colombard, Gascony (£2–2.50).
Liebfraumilch (£2–2.50).
Muscadet sur Lie (£2.50–3).

REDS

Bulgarian Cabernet Sauvignon (£2–2.50).
Vaucluse (£–2).
Mountain Cabernet (£3+).
Crozes-Hermitage (£2.50–3).
Cooks New Zealand Red (£2.50–3).
Good South African, Australian and Californians (£3+).
Clarets reasonably priced for the quality (£3+).

SPARKLING WINES

German Sekt (£2.50–3).
Pol Pasquier Champagne (£3+).

SHERRY

Geraldia (£2.50–3).

PORT

Royal Oporto '82 (£3+).

GALLEON

See the range from Augustus Barnett.

GATEWAY

WHITES

Lambrusco (£–2).
Anjou Blanc (£–2).
Muscadet (£–2). Dry.
Soave (£–2). Dry.
Lutomer Laski Riesling (£–2).
Liebfraumilch $1\frac{1}{2}$ litres (£3+).

REDS

Spanish Red (£–2).
Corrida (£–2).
Lambrusco (£–2).
Valpolicella (£–2).
Côtes du Rhône (£2–2.50).
Chianti Classico (£2–2.50).

SWEET WINE

Premières Côtes de Bordeaux (£2–2.50).

SPARKLING WINES

Vin Mousseux (£2.50–3).
Moscato Spumante (£2.50–3).
Brut de Listel (£3+).
Asti Spumante, Martini (£3+).
Charles Heidsieck Champagne (£3+).

SHERRY

QC British (£–2).
Monte Cristo (£2–2.50).

PORT

Cockburn's Fine Old Ruby (£3+).

GOUGH BROTHERS

WHITES

French Les Forges (£–2).
Liebfraumilch (£–2).
Cloberg Laski Riesling (£–2).
Muscadet (£2–2.50).
Bulgarian and Italianski Riesling (£2–2.50).
Yugoslavian Gewurtztraminer (£2–2.50).

REDS

French Les Forges (£–2).
Hungarian Cabernet Sauvignon (£–2).
Hungarian Pinot Noir (£–2).
Bulgarian Mehana and Cabernet Sauvignon (£–2).
Côtes du Rhône (£–2).
Syrah Vin de Pays (£2–2.50).
Bulls Blood (£2–2.50).
Buzet (£3+).
Israeli Palwin No. 10.
Rioja Añares (£2–2.50).

SWEET WINES

Premières Côtes de Bordeaux (£2.50–3).
Sauternes (£3+).

SPARKLING WINES

Cavalier (£2–2.50).
Sparkling Saumur (£3+).
Mercier Champagne (£3+).

SHERRY

Gun Dog (£2.50–3).

PORT

Sandeman's range (£3+).

GRANDWAYS

WHITES

Muscadet (£–2). Dry.
Soave (£–2). Dry.
Lambrusco (£–2).
Don Cortez (£–2). Dry to sweet.
Lutomer Laski Riesling (£–2).
Mateus (£2–2.50).
Black Tower (£2–2.50).
Blue Nun (£2.50–3).

REDS

Lambrusco (£–2).
Côtes du Roussillon (£–2).
Le Patron (£–2).
Minervois (£–2).
Capricco (Bolzano) ($1\frac{1}{2}$ litres) (£3+).
Château Tour Prignac (£3+).

SWEET WINE

Barsac (£3+).

SPARKLING WINES

Framar Spumante (£2–2.50).
Veuve Amiot, Sparkling Saumur (£3+).

SHERRY

QC range (£–2).
Emva Cream (£2–2.50).
Croft Original (£3+).

PORT

Cockburn's and Sandeman's Ruby (£3+).

HILLARDS

WHITES

Liebfraumilch (£–2).
Niersteiner (£–2).
Piesporter (£2–2.50).
British Country Manor and Chambard (£–2).

REDS

Château Clos l'Eglise (Bordeaux Superior) (£2.50–3).

SPARKLING WINES

Tiffany (British) (£2–2.50).
Moscato Spumante (£2.50–3).
Asti Spumante Martini (£2.50–3).
Veuve du Vernay (£3+).

HINTONS

They sell their own selection and a restricted range of 'Argyl' and 'Presto' brands.

JOHN SARSON WINES/JOHN SARSON AND SON LTD./BOTTLES/G.B. WINES/QUEEN'S CELLARS/RUTLAND VINTNERS

WHITES

Bulgarian Mehana Chardonnay and Riesling (£−2).
Gold Vine Euroblend (£−2).
Liebfraumilch 'Kellergeist' (£2−2.50).
Alouette and La Seine litres of French Table Wine (£2.50−3).
Sancerre '84 (£3+).

REDS

Bulgarian Mehana Cabernet Sauvignon (£−2).
Alouette and La Seine litres of French Table Wine (£2.50−3).
Chateau Patache d'Aux '78 (£3+).
Château La Tour St. Bonnet (£3+).
Château Citran (£3+).
Château Cantenac Brown '82 (£3+).

SWEET WINES

Premières Côtes de Bordeaux (£2.50−3).
Sauternes and Barsac (£3+).

SPARKLING WINES

Cavalier (£3+).
Etienne Dumont Champagne (£3+).

SHERRY

Fontera range (£3+).

Shippers Choice (£3+).
A fine range of Vintage Ports (£3+).

JAMES MELLOR WINES/MELLOR & PATISON/THE VINEYARD

WHITES

Vin Blanc (£−2). Dry.
Lambrusco Bianco (£−2).
Liebfraumilch (£2−2.50).
'House Wine' Euroblend (£2.50−3 a litre).
Chablis '83. Dry (£3+).
Clos du Château, Château de Meursault '81 (£3+). Dry.

REDS

Vin Rouge (£−2).

SWEET WINE

Sauternes (£3+).

SPARKLING WINES

Moscato Spumante (£2.50−3).
Arlit Carte Blanche Champagne (£3+).

SHERRY

British Spring Grove (£2−2.50).

PORT

Good vintage range. Dow's and Taylor's (£3+).

JULIAN FLOOK

WHITES

Liebfraumilch (£–2).
Liebfraumilch Helenhof (£–2).
Euroblend St. Helena (£–2).
Mosel Longnicher Probsberg Kabinet (£2.50–3).

REDS

Minervois (£–2).
Roussillon (£–2).
Costières du Gard (£2–2.50).

SWEET WHITE WINE

Première Côtes de Bordeaux (£2.50–3).

SPARKLING WINES

Ackerman Sparkling Saumur (£3+).
Alain Gerbert Rosé (£3+).

SHERRY

Howells of Bristol range (£2.50–3).

PORT

Cockburn's, Sandeman's and Taylor's (£3+).

KWIK-SAVE

WHITES

Liebfraumilch (£–2).
Lambrusco (£–2).
Soave (£–2). Dry.
Crown of Crowns and Blue Nun (£2.50–3).

REDS

Lambrusco (£–2).
Bulls Blood (£2–2.50).
Le Piat d'Or (£2–2.50).
Cooks New Zealand Muller Thurgau and Gewurtztraminer
  (£2.50–3).

SWEET WINE

Hirondelle and Don Cortez (£–2).

SPARKLING WINES

Moscato Spumante (£2–2.50).
Lanson Champagne (£3+).

SHERRY

British QC (£–2).
Cyprus Mosaic Cream (£2–2.50).

PORT

Cockburn's Fine Old Ruby (£3+).

LAY & WHEELER

WHITES

Muscadet (£2–2.50). Dry.
Liebfraumilch (£2–2.50).
Côtes de Gascogne, Colombard (£2–2.50). Dry.
Alsace Blanck's Sylvaner Reserve (£3+). Dry.
Jurançon Blanc de Blancs (£2.50–3). Dry.
Langham's and New Hall (English) (£3+).

REDS

Balkan Selection Cabernet Sauvignon (£2–2.50).
Cabernet Rouge de Haut Poitou (£2.50–3).
Côtes du Rhône (£2.50–3).

SWEET WINES

Jurancon Quadri Centenaire (£3+).
Tokay (£3+).

SPARKLING WINES

Rôbe d'Or (£3+).
Ellner Champagne (£3+).

SHERRY

Lay & Wheeler Oyster Catcher Amontillado (£3+).
Oloroso Especial Hidalgo (£3+).

PORT

Churchill Vintage Character (£3+).
Extensive range of Vintage Ports (£3+).

LIQUORSAVE/ NORTH-WEST VINTNERS/ WINTERSCHLADEN

WHITES

Liebfraumilch (£−2).
French Table Wine (£−2).
Piesporter (£2−2.50).

REDS

Lambrusco (£−2).
Côtes du Roussillon (£−2).

126

SWEET WINE

Don Cortez (£−2).

SPARKLING WINES

Moscato Spumante (£2−2.50).
Champagne Albert Ettienne (£3+).

SHERRY

Varela range (£2.50−3).

PORT

Triple Crown (£3+).

LITTLEWOODS

WHITES

Liebfraumilch (£−2).
French Table (£−2).
Bulgarian Sauvignon Blanc (£−2).
Tarona (Valencia) (£−2).
Lambrusco (£−2).
Piesporter Michelberg (£2−2.50).
Blue Nun (£2.50−3).

REDS

Tarona (£−2).
Corbières (£−2).
Minervois (£−2).
Ventoux (£−2).
Le Piat d'Or (£2.50−3).

SWEET WINE

Sweet Tarona (£−2).

SPARKLING WINES

Riviera Asti Spumarte (£2–2.50).
Gancia Spumante (£3+).
Champagne Marguerite Christal (£3+).

SHERRY

Club Royal (£–2).
Montilla (£–2).
Emva Cream (Cyprus) (£2.50–3).

PORT

Club Royal Fine Old Ruby (£3+).
Cockburn's Special Reserve (£3+).

LO-COST

WHITES

Tafelwein Euroblend Winzerschoppen (£–2).
Liebfraumilch Siebrand (£–2).
Blue Nun (£2.50–3).

REDS

Don Cortez (£–2).
Beaujolais 'Argyl' or 'Presto' (£2–2.50).
Chianti (£–2).

SPARKLING WINE

String of Pearls (Cider, looking like Champagne) (£–2).

SHERRY

Old England (British) (£–2).
The Domecq range (£3+).

PORT

Croft Triple Crown (£3+).

MACE LINE

Mace, and some Wavy line shops will sell a range of wines related to Budgen – though the prices may be different.

MAJESTIC WINE WAREHOUSES (WINES BY THE CASE)

With their high rate of case turnover, Majestic change lines more rapidly than most.

WHITES

Bulgarian Chardonnay (£−2).
Liebfraumilch (£−2).
Chenin Blanc (£−2). Dry.
Muscadet '84 (£−2). Dry.
Tondonia Rioja Blanco '75 (£2.50−3). Dry.
Cune Monopole '82 (£2.50−3). Dry.
Mâcon Villages (£2.50−3). Dry.
Bourgogne Aligoté (£2.50−3). Dry.
Geoffrey Roberts Reserve White Californian (£2.50−3).
Bruisyard St. Peter (English) (£2.50−3).
Adgestone (English) (£2.50−3).
Six different Chablis.
Tiefenbonner '84 (£3+).

REDS

Bulgarian Merlot, Cabernet Sauvignon and Red (all £−2).
Côtes du Rhône (£−2).
Domaine du Pech d'André (Minervois) (£−2).
Domaine de l'Abbaye de Valmagne '81 (£2−2.50).
Monte Real (£2.50−3).

Torres Coronas '81 (£2.50–3).
Bulgarian Sakar Mountain (£2.50–3).
Mavrud (£2.50–3).
Geoffrey Roberts Reserve Californian Red (£2.50–3).

SWEET WINE

Moscato d'Asti '83 (£2.50–3).
Samos Muscat (£3+).

SPARKLING WINES

Selection of Champagnes (£3+).
Cavalier (£2–2.50).
Moscato Spumante (£2.50–3).

SHERRY

Perez Barquero Montilla (£–2).
Emilio Lustau Oloroso (very sweet) (£2.50–3).
Garvey Fino San Patricio (£3+).

PORT

Graham's Late Bottled Vintage '78.

MARKS & SPENCER

WHITES

Lambrusco (£–2).
Côtes du Gascogne (£2–2.50). Dry.
Liebfraumilch (£2–2.50).
Château Petit Moulin '85 (£2.50–3). Dry.
Chablis '84 (£3+). Dry.

REDS AND ROSÉ

Lambrusco (£–2).
Côtes du Rhône, Les Trois Oratoires (£2.50–3).

Rosé d'Anjou (£2.50–3 a litre).
Romeral Rioja litres and its Gran Reserva quality (£2.50–3).
French Full Red (from Roussillon) in litres (£3+).

SPARKLING WINES

Asti Spumante (£3+).
Champagne (£3+).

SHERRY

Marks and Spencer Sherries (£3+).

PORT

Marks and Spencer Port (£3+).

MORRISONS

WHITES

Liebfraumilch (£–2).
Pfeiffer Euroblend (£–2).
Lambrusco (£–2).
Listel sur Lie (£–2). Dry.

REDS

Corbières (£–2).
Fitou (£2–2.50).
Le Piat d'Or (£2.50–3).
The Burgundies and Beaujolais of Georges Duboeuf (£3+).

SPARKLING WINES

Moscato Ambra (£2.50–3).
Henri Marcel Dry French (£2.50–3).
Asti Spumante Martini (£3+).

MORRIS'S WINE STORES

WHITES

Liebfraumilch (£−2).
bulgarian Riesling (£2−2.50).
Bulgarian Chardonnay (£2−2.50). Dry.
Greek Domestica (£2.50−3).
Greek Retsina (£2.50−3).
Piesporter (£2.50−3).

REDS

Bulgarian Cabernet Sauvignon (£2−2.50).
Greek Domestica (£2.50−3).
Côtes du Rhône Vacqueyras (£2.50−3).
Beaujolais Villages, Pichet (£3+).
St. Joseph '82, De Valouit (£3+).
Chianti Rufina 'Remole' Frescobaldi (£3+).

SWEET WINE

Spanish Castillo de Lira (£−2).

SPARKLING WINES

Robe d'Or (£3+).
Sparkling Saumur (£3+).

SHERRY

Garvey (£3+).

PORT

Graham's Late Bottled Vintage '78 (£3+).

NORMANS

WHITES

Liebfraumilch (£−2).
Caves de Massé French Table White (£−2).
Veronese (£−2).
Soave (£−2).
Frascati (£2−2.50).

REDS

Lambrusco (£−2).
Caves de Massé French Table Red (£−2).
Veronese (£−2).
Valpolicella (£−2).
Côtes du Roussillon (£2−2.50).
Beaujolais (£2.50−3).

ODDBINS

WHITES

Liebfraumilch (£−2).
Soave Fabiano (£−2).
Drathen Tafelwein Euroblend (£−2).
Bulgarian Chardonnay (£−2). Dry.
Muscadet (£2.50−3). Dry.
Several good Alsace wines in the (£2.50−3) range.
New Zealand Montana Chardonnay and Sauvignon Blanc (£3+). Dry.
English Lamberhurst (£3+).

REDS

Bulgarian Mehana (£−2).
Hungarian Cabernet Sauvignon and Pinot Noir (£−2).
Valpolicella (£−2).

Corbières (£2–2.50).
Beaujolais (£2–2.50).
Moroccan Tarik (£2–2.50).
Quinta do Convento '76 (£2–2.50).
Minervois Château de Donjon (£2–2.50).
Côtes du Rhône Bernard (£2–2.50).
Barbera d'Asti (£2.50–3).
Rosemount Coonawarra Shiraz '84 (£3+).
Garrafeira Caves Velhas '74 (£3+).
Château d'Archambeau '84 (Graves) (£3+).

SWEET WINE

St. Croix du Mont '73 (£3+).

SPARKLING WINES

Cavalier Blanc de Blancs (£2.50–3).
Mumm Champagne (£3+).

SHERRY

Barbadillo Fino (£2.50–3).
Barbadillo Amontillado (£2.50–3).

PORT

Guimaraens Fine Old Vintage Character (£3+).
Graham's Late Bottled Vintage (£3+).

PEATLING & CAWDRON

WHITES

Liebfraumilch (£2–2.50).
Vin de Table (£–2).
Pettau Yugoslav Laski Riesling (£–2).
Peatling's Euroblend (£–2).

Gros Plant (£2.50–3).
Vin de Pays Côtes de Gascogne '84 (£2–2.50).
English Chilford Hundred and Pulham(£3+).

REDS

Peatling's French Red (£–2).
Fitou (£2–2.50).
Peatling's Claret (£2.50–3).
Côtes du Rhône Domaine de la Renjardière '84 (£3+).
Côtes de Buzet (£3+).
Château de May '78 and '81 (Graves) (£3+).
Santa Digna, Miguel Torres (Chilean) (£3+).

SWEET WINE

Beaumes de Venise (£3+).

SPARKLING WINES

Peatling & Cawdron French Sparkling (£3+).
Champagne Brusson Père & Fils (£3+).

SHERRY

Peatling & Cawdron Sherries (£3+).
Garvey Fino San Patricio (£3+) available at some branches.

PORT

Peatling & Cawdron Port (£2.50–3).

PETER DOMINIC

WHITES

Yugoslav Cloberg (£–2).
Pedrotti Lambrusco (£–2).
Spanish White (£–2). Dry.

Soave Villa Belvedere (£−2). Dry.
Liebfraumilch St. Dominic (£−2).
Bulgarian Pinot Chardonnay (£−2). Dry.
Yugoslav Lutomer, Gewurtztraminer and Tiger Milk (£2−2.50).
Hungarian Cloberg (£2−2.50).
Greek Retsina and Domestica (£2.50−3).
Cooks New Zealand White (£2.50−3). Dry.
Alsace Pinot Blanc (£2.50−3). Dry.
Lamberhurst English (£2.50−3).
Alsace Riesling and Gewurtztraminer (£3+).
Carr Taylor English (£3+).
Australian Rosemount Chardonnay (£3+). Dry.
Urzinger Schwarzlay Riesling Kabinet Mosel '83 (£3+).
Ockfener Bockelheim Auslese '83 (£3+).

REDS

Bulgarian Cabernet Sauvignon and Merlot (£−2).
Pedrotti Lambrusco (£−2).
Beaujolais Nouveau (£−2).
Spanish Red (£−2).
Navarra Castillo del Ebro (£−2).
Algerian Red Infuriator (£2.50−3).
Claret (£2.50−3).
Rosso Conero (£2.50−3).
Lagunilla Rioja (£2.50−3).
Bulgarian Mavrud (£2.50−3).
Cooks New Zealand Red (£2.50−3).
Dão Tinto (Portugal) (£2.50−3).
Geisweiler's Burgundy, Cuvée 18ème Siècle (£3+).
Château Terrey Gros Caillou '79 (£3+).
Domecq Domain Rioja (£3+).
Lebanon Château Musar (£3+).

SWEET WINES

Château la Brie '81 Monbazillac (£3+).
Kreuznacher Forst Riesling Auslese '76 (£3+).

SPARKLING WINES

Dopff Cuvée Extra Crémant d'Alsace (£3+).
Lambert Blanc de Blanc Champagne (£3+).
Blanquette de Limoux (£3+).
Crémant de Loire (£3+).
Le Piat Crystal (£3+).

SHERRY

Conde de la Cortina Montilla (£−2).
Old England British (£2−2.50).
Dominicus Fino (£2.50−3).
La Ina (£3+).

PORT AND MADEIRA

Croft Fine Ruby (£3+).
Noval LB (£3+).
Blandy's Madeira Duke of ... series – Sercial, Verdelho, Bual
   and Malmsey (£3+).

PRESTO

WHITES

Tafelwein Euroblend (£−2).
Liebfraumilch (£−2).
Lambrusco (£−2).
Country Manor Perry (£−2).
Lutomer Laski Riesling (£−2).
Presto Hock (£−2).
Muscadet (£2−2.50). Dry.
Blue Nun (£2.50−3).

REDS AND ROSÉ

Lambrusco (£−2).
Presto Chianti (£−2).
Claret (£2−2.50).
Mateus Rosé (£2−2.50).

SPARKLING WINES

Moscato Spumante (£2–2.50).
Presto Champagne (£3+).

SHERRY

Presto British (£–2).
Presto Spanish (£2.50–3).
Gonzales Byass Elegante Sherries (£3+).

PORT

Presto Ruby (£2.50–3).
Cockburn's Special Reserve (£3+).

ROBERTS/COOPER

WHITES

Muscadet (£–2). Dry.
Bereich Nierstein (£–2).
Cloberg Laski Riesling (£–2).
Blue Nun and Black Tower (£2.50–3).
Piesporter Michelsberg (£2.50–3).

REDS

Lambrusco (£–2).
Bardolino (£–2).
Monte Campo Red (£–2).
Cloberg Red (£–2).
Côtes du Rhône Château de la Ramière '83 (£2.50–3).
Olarra Red Rioja (£2.50–3).
Fleurie Pasquier Desvignes (£3+).

SWEET WINE

Sauternes Eschenauer (£3+).

SPARKLING WINES

Moscato Spumante (£2–2.50).
Greyman (French) (£3+).
Piper Heidsieck Champagne (£3+).

SHERRY

Litres of Cyprus Lysander Medium (£3+).

PORT

Sandeman's Ruby (£3+).

SAFEWAY

WHITES

Liebfraumilch (£–2).
Lutomer Laski Riesling (£–2).
Hungarian Tramini (£–2).
Yugoslav Gewurtztraminer (£–2).
Lamberhurst English (£2–2.50).
Sylvaner d'Alsace (£2–2.50).
Muscadet (£2–2.50). Dry.
Piesporter Michelsberg (£2.50–3).
Ruffino Orvieto Classico '84 (£2.50–3).
Fontana Candida Frascati (£2.50–3).

REDS

Hungarian Merlot (£–2).
Vino de Mesa (£–2).
Côtes du Luberon (£–2).
Fitou (£2–2.50).
Israeli Carmel (£2–2.50).
Ruffino Chianti Classico Aziano '83 (£2.50–3).
Bourgogne Rouge (£2.50–3).
Crozes-Hermitage (£3+).
Saint Joseph '83 (£3+).
Raimat Abadia (£3+).

SWEET WINES

Moscatel de Valencia (£2–2.50).
Marsala (£2.50–3).
Château du Pick (Sauternes) (£3+).

SPARKLING WINES

Sparkling Saumur (£3+).
Spanish Cava (£3+).

SHERRY

Safeway (own brand) (£3+).

PORT AND MADEIRA

Cockburn's Special Reserve (£3+).
Blandy's Duke of Clarence Rich Malmsey (Madeira) (£3+).

SAINSBURY'S

WHITES

White Euroblend (£–2).
Laski Riesling (£–2).
Liebfraumilch (£–2).
Muscadet (£2–2.50). Dry.
Soave (£–2). Dry.
White Bergerac (£–2). Dry.
Alsace Pinot Blanc and Sylvaner (£2–2.50). Dry.
Californian White (£2–2.50).
Alsace Gewurtztraminer (£3+).

REDS

Raboso del Veneto (£–2).
Tonino (Sicily) (£–2).
Lambrusco (£–2).
Claret (£2–2.50).

Californian Red (£2–2.50).
Crozes-Hermitage (£2–2.50).
Buzet (£2–2.50).
Bergerac (£2–2.50).
Château de Gourgazaud, Minervois, Magnum (£3+).
Quinta de Bacalhôa (Portugal) (£3+).

SWEET WINES

Clos St. Georges (£3+).
Muscat Beaumes de Venise (£3+).

SPARKLING WINES

Sparkling Saumur (£3+).
Sainsbury's Champagne (£3+).

SHERRY

Sainsbury's Montilla (£2–2.50).
Sainsbury's dry Manzanilla (£2.50–3).
Harvey's Bristol Cream (£3+).

PORT AND MADEIRA

Sainsbury's Ruby and Tawny (£3+).
Sainsbury's Madeira (£3+).

SAVERITE

WHITES

Liebfraumilch (£–2).
Lutomer Laski Riesling (£–2).
Soave (£–2). Dry.
Piesporter (£2–2.50).
Muscadet (£2–2.50). Dry.

REDS AND ROSÉ

Lambrusco (£–2).

Valpolicella (£−2).
Médoc (£2−2.50).
Côtes du Rhône (£2−2.50).
Mateus Rosé (£2.50−3).

SPARKLING WINES

Moscato Spumante (£2−2.50).
Sparkling Blue Nun (£3+).

SHERRY

NISA range (£2.50−3).
Harvey's Bristol Cream (£3+).
Garvey Fino San Patricio (£3+).

PORT

Sandeman's Founders Reserve (£3+).
Cockburn's Ruby (£3+).

SHERSTON WINE COMPANY

WHITES

St. Urban Euroblend (£−2).
Soave (£2−2.50). Dry.
Ochoa White '83 (£2−2.50). Dry.
Los Palcos (£2−2.50). Dry.
Monopole. Dry. Rioja (£3+).
Marques de Caceres. Dry. Rioja (£3+).
Marques de Murrieta. Dry. Rioja. (£3+)
English Bruisyard St. Peter, Wraxall and Sherston Earl (£3+).

REDS

Rivarey (£2.50−3). Rioja.
El Coto (£2.50−3). Rioja.
Marques de Riscal (£3+). Rioja.

142

Raimat Abadia (£3+).
Muga (£3+). Rioja.

SWEET WINE
Yugoslav Red Muscat Hamburg (£2–2.50).

SPARKLING WINES
Conde de Caralt Brut Cava (£3+).
Castellenblanch Rosé (£3+).

SHERRY
La Guita Manzanilla (£3+).
La Serna Old Amontillado (£3+).

PORT
Churchill Vintage Character (£3+).

SHOPPERS PARADISE

WHITES
Alfresco Spanish (£–2).
Liebfraumilch (£–2).
Mosel Deutcher Tafelwein (£–2).
Lutomer Laski Riesling (£–2).
Soave (£–2). Dry.
Rendezvous Vin Blanc (medium) (£–2).
Chambard and Country Manor Perry (British) (£–2).

REDS
Lambrusco (£–2).
Alfresco Spanish (£–2).
Valpolicella (£–2).
Le Piat d'Or (£2–2.50).

SWEET WINE
Alfresco Spanish (£–2).

SPARKLING WINE

La Strada Spumante (£2–2.50).

SHERRY

Diez Amontillado (£–2).
Gold Dust British (£–2).
Mandola Amontillado (Fine Fare Ltd.) (£2–2.50).

PORT

Cockburn's (£3+).

SPAR

The selection of wines in **Spar** outlets is chosen by each individual retailer from an extensive list.

WHITES

Liebfraumilch.
Siebrand Winzerschoppen Euroblend.
White Lambrusco.
Mosel Tafelwein.
Lutomer Laski Riesling.
Piesporter.

REDS

Lambrusco.
Don Cortez.
Country Carafe (British).
British Concorde and Country Manor Perry.
Le Piat d'Or.

SWEET WINE

Don Cortez.

SPARKLING WINES

Moscato Spumante.
Veuve du Vernay.

SHERRY

Spar British.
Cyprus Emva Cream.
Gonzalez Byass and Harvey's range.

PORT

Cockburn's Ruby.

TANNERS

WHITES

Sonnenstubchen Euroblend Tafelwein (£−2).
Bulgarian Riesling (£−2).
Liebfraumilch (£2−2.50).
Bernkasteler Kurfurstlay '84 (£2.50−3).
Pinot Grigio (Del' Alto Adige − Santa Marguerita) (£3+). Dry.
Puilly Fumé (£3+). Dry.
English Three Choirs, Newhall's, Broadfield Court and Adgestone (£3+).
Franken Wine Wurtzberger Stein Riesling Kabinet '82 (all £3+). Dry.

REDS

Tanners Bulgarian Cabernet Sauvignon (£−2).
Tanners Claret (£2.50−3).
Tanners Pinot Noir Burgundy (£3+).
Château Musar (£3+).
Chilean Vina Linderos '82 (£3+).
Large range of Australian, South African, New Zealand and Californian wines (£3+).
Châteauneuf du Pape, Vieux Télégraphe '81, '82 and '83 (£3+).

SWEET WINES

Jurançon Cuvee Quadri Centenaire − Moelleux (£3+).
Beaumes de Venise (£3+).
Sweet Loire Moulin Touchais '55 and '69 (£3+).

SPARKLING WINES

Rôbe d'Or (£2.50–3).
Tanners Brut Reserve (£3+).

SHERRY

Tanners Own Brands (£2.50–3).

PORT AND MADEIRA

Patrono Fine Old Ruby (£3+).
Rutherford & Miles, Cossárt Gordon and Blandy's Madeiras
   (£3+).

TATES

WHITES

Lutomer Laski Riesling (£–2).
Liebfraumilch (£2–2.50).
Lambrusco (£2–2.50).
Piesporter (£2–2.50).

REDS

Lambrusco (£2–2.50).
Cordier (£2.50–3 a litre).
Le Piat d'Or and Piat Beaujolais (£3+).

SWEET WINES

Cordier (£2.50–3 a litre).
La Flora Sweet Bordeaux (£2.50–3).

SPARKLING WINES

Veuve du Vernay (£3+).
Le Piat Crystal (£3+).

SHERRY

Montilla (£2–2.50).
Croft (£3+).

PORT

Cockburn's and Noval LB (£3+).

TESCO

WHITES

Liebfraumilch (£–2).
Lutomer Laski Riesling (£2–2.50).
Bulgarian Welsch Riesling (£–2).
Valdadige Bianco (£–2). Dry.
Soave (£–2). Dry.
Muscadet (£2–2.50). Dry.
Orvieto (£2–2.50).
St. Edmund English (£2–2.50).
Alsace Gewurtztraminer (£3+).
Chablis (£3+). Dry.

REDS

Côtes du Rhône (£2–2.50).
Barbaresco (£3+).
Anjou Rouge (£–2).
Lago di Caldaro (£–2).
Lambrusco di Sorbara (£–2).
Israeli ein Gedi (£–2).
Dão (£2–2.50).
Syrah (£2–2.50).
Gran Feudo Navarra (£2–2.50).
Bergerac (£2–2.50).
Vina Lanaga Rioja '82 (£2–2.50).
Israeli Cabernet Sauvignon (£2–2.50).
Bourgogne Rouge (£3+).
Châteauneuf du Pape Les Arnevels (£3+).

SWEET WINE
Monbazillac (£2–2.50).

SPARKLING WINES
Moscato Spumante (£2.50–3).
Sparkling Saumur (£3+).

SHERRY
Premium Fino and Amontillado (£2.50–3).

PORT
Taylor's Late Bottled Vintage '78 (£3+).
Tesco's Ruby (£3+).
Tesco Fine Old Vintage Character (£3+).

THRESHERS

WHITES
Liebfraumilch (£2.50–3).
Balkan Cellar (£–2).
Corrida (£–2).
White Dão (£2–2.50).
Hock and Mosel (£2–2.50).
Yugoslav Cloberg and Lutomer Laski Riesling (£2–2.50).
South African KWV Chenin Blanc (£2–2.50).

REDS
Corrida (£–2).
Balkan Cellar (£–2).
Dão Dom Ferraz (£2–2.50).
Fitou (£2–2.50).
Domecq Vina Eguia '81 (£2.50–3).
South African KWV Rooderberg (£2.50–3) and Pinotage
    (£2.50–3).
Marques de Cáceres Rioja (£3+).

SWEET WINES

Boulevard (£−2).
Premières Côtes de Bordeaux (£2.50−3).
Monbazillac (£3+).

SPARKLING WINES

Veuve du Vernay (£3+).
Thirteen Champagnes (£3+).

SHERRY

Threshers own brand of Cyprus Sherry (£2.50−3).
Domecq Double Century (£3+).

PORT

Ferreira Ruby and Tawny (£3+).

TOWNEND

WHITES

Vin Ordinaire Mosel (£−2).
Lutomer Riesling (£−2).
Baden Prince (£2−2.50).
Australian Old Triangle Riesling '85 (£2.50−3).
Baden Ortenau Riesling '82 (£2.50−3).
Cooks New Zealand Chenin Blanc (£2.50−3).
English Lamberhurst (£2.50−3).

REDS

Bulgarian Cabernet Sauvignon and Merlot (£2−2.50).
Côtes du Rhône (£2−2.50).
Rioja Arpillera (in a sack) (£2−2.50).
Cooks New Zealand Cabernet Sauvignon (£2.50−3).
Château Brondeau (£2.50−3).
Château Reynon (£2.50−3).
Crozes-Hermitage '82 (£3+).
Pomerol Feytit Clinet '81 (£3+).

SWEET WINE
Château des Tours (£2.50–3).

SPARKLING WINES
Rôbe d'Or (£2–2.50).
Sparkling Saumur (£3+).

SHERRY
The Wisdom and Warter range (£2–2.50).

PORT
Sportsman, Directors' Bin (£3+).

UNWINS

WHITES
Blanc de Blancs (£2–2.50).
Liebfraumilch (£2–2.50).
Piemontello (just fizzy) (£2–2.50).
Muscadet (£2–2.50). Dry.
Bourgogne Aligoté (£3+). Dry.
Lamberhurst English. (£2.50–3).
Rosemount Chardonnay (Australian) (£3+).
KWV South African wines. Chenin Blanc (£3+).

REDS
Rouge de France (£–2).
Côtes du Roussillon (£2–2.50).
Corbières (£2–2.50).
Cahors (£2.50–3).
Bordeaux Rouge (£3+).
Château le Peyrat '84 Graves (£3+).
Château Musar (£3+).

SWEET WINE

Château Gaillon '83, St. Croix du Mont (£2.50–3).

SPARKLING WINES

Baron d'Arcel (£3+).
Sparkling Saumur (£3+).

SHERRY

Dry Sack (£3+).
Double Century Oloroso (£3+).

PORT

Cockburn's Ruby (£3+).

VG

WHITES

Liebfraumilch (£–2).
Lutomer Laski Riesling (£–2).
Don Cortez (£–2).
Yugoslavian Tiger Milk (£–2). (Telcher Bros.).
Blanc de Blancs Fruits de Mer (£–2). Dry.
Lambrusco (£–2).
Hirondelle (£–2).
Rioja Marques de Ciria (£2–2.50). Dry.
Frascati (£2.50–3). Dry.
Le Piat d'Or (£2.50–3).

REDS

Valpolicella (£–2).
Lambrusco (£–2).
Conde Bel and Ellauri Rioja (£2–2.50).
Côtes du Rhône, Domaine de l'Eonne (£2–2.50).
Claret '83 (£2.50–3).
Californian Carafe (£2.50–3).

SWEET WINE

Graves Superior (£3+).

SPARKLING WINES

Moscato Spumante (£2–2.50).
Gancia Spumante (£3+).
Asti Spumante (£3+).

SHERRY

Old England British (£–2).
Emva Cream Cyprus (£2–2.50).
Osborne (£2.50–3).

PORT

Cockburn's Fine Old Ruby (£3+).

THE VICTORIA WINE COMPANY

WHITES

Don Cortez (£–2).
Kronen Tafelwein Euroblend (£–2).
Laski Riesling (£–2).
Special Liebfraumilch (£–2).
Piemontello (just fizzy) (£2–2.50).
South African Stellenberg Chenin Blanc (£–2).
Grunne Kanne Liebfraumilch (£3+).
Morio Muskat (£3+).
Roussillon (£2.50–3). Dry.
Rosemount Australian Chardonnay (£3+). Dry.

REDS

Yugoslavian Red (£–2).
Don Cortez (£–2).
Côtes du Rhône (£2–2.50).

Banda Azul Rioja (£2.50–3).
Stellenberg Roodekeur (£2–2.50).
Carafe Cabernet Sauvignon (£2.50–3).
Nicholas Vieux Ceps (£3+).
Côtes du Roussillon (£2.50–3).
Californian Franzia (£3+).
The Burgundies of Louis Jadot (£3+).
Raimat Abadia 1982 (£3+).

SWEET WINE

Muscat (£2.50–3).

SPARKLING WINES

Pigalle (£2.50–3).
Veuve du Vernay (£3+).
Sparkling Saumur (£3+).

SHERRY

Olé range (£2.50–3).
Harvey's Bristol Cream (£3+).

PORT

Taylor's '79 Late Bottled Vintage (£3+).
Conference Fine Old Ruby (£3+).
Cockburn's Late Bottled '80 (£3+).

WAITROSE

WHITES

Liebfraumilch (£–2).
Lutomer Laski Riesling (£–2).
Vin de Pays Côtes de Gascogne (£–2). Dry.
White Lambrusco (£2–2.50).
Romanian Riesling de Banat (£–2).
Hock Deutcher Tafelwein (£–2).
Carafe White (Sardinia) (£2–2.50 a litre). Dry.

Culemborg Colombar, South African (£−2).
Château Senailhac (£2−2.50). Dry.
Corinth Retsina (£2−2.50).
Soave (£−2). Dry.
Cooks New Zealand White (£2.50−3). Dry.
Alsace Riesling and Gewurtztraminer (£2.50−3).
South Tyrol Gewurtztraminer (£3+).
Château Moncontour '83 (£3+). Demi-sec.
Frascati (£2.50−3). Dry.
Carr Taylor Reichensteiner '83 (£2.50−3).
English Fonthill (£3+).
Australian Houghton Supreme (£3+).
Chablis '84 (£3+).
Californian North Coast Cellars Chenin Blanc (£3+).
Château de Meursault (£3+).

REDS

Hungarian Red (£2.50−3 a litre).
Bulgarian Red (£−2).
Buzet (£2−2.50).
Bulgarian Cabernet Sauvignon (£−2).
Culemborg Pinotage, South African (£−2).
Valpolicella (£−2).
Lambrusco (£2−2.50).
Greek Apollo (£−2).
Carafe Red (Sardinia) (£2−2.50 a litre).
Gran Feudo (Navarra) (£2−2.50).
Claret (£2−2.50).
Dão (£2−2.50).
Fitou (£2−2.50).
Beaujolais Villages (£2.50−3).
Rioja Lancorta (£2.50−3).
Cooks New Zealand Red (£2.50−3).
Tinto da Anfora (£2.50−3).
Crozes-Hermitage, Caves des Clairmonts (£3+).
Californian Fetzer Zinfandel (£3+).
Venegazzu '80 (£3+).
Château Musar (£3+).
Chilean Concho y Toro (£2.50−3).

SWEET WINES

Premières Côtes de Bordeaux (£2–2.50).
Jurançon Moelleux Quadri-Centenaire (£2.50–3).
Château Septy, Monbazillac (£3+).

SPARKLING WINES

Blanquette de Limoux (£3+).
Waitrose Champagne (£3+).
Crémant d'Alsace (Dopff) (£3+).

SHERRY

Montilla (£2–2.50).
South African Sherry (£2–2.50).
Barbadillo Manzanilla (£3+).

PORT

Waitrose Fine Ruby (£3+).
Fonseca Bin 27 (£3+).

WALTER WILLSON AND THOMAS PATTERSON

WHITES

Liebfraumilch (£–2).
Don Cortez (£–2).
Lutomer Laski Riesling (£–2).
Piesporter (£2–2.50).

REDS

Don Cortez (£–2).
Romanian Cabernet Sauvignon (£2–2.50).

Côtes du Rhône (Marson & Natier) (£2–2.50).
Valpolicella Ambra (£2–2.50).

SWEET WINES

La Flora Blanche (£2–2.50).
Sweet White Bordeaux (£2–2.50).

SPARKLING WINES

Moscato Spumante (£2–2.50).
Le Piat Crystal (£3+).

SHERRY

Harvey's (£3+).

PORT

Cockburn's Ruby (£3+).

WHYNOT WINE WAREHOUSES

Wines by the case.

WHITES

Vin de Pays Charantais (£–2). Dry.
Bulgarian Chardonnay (£–2).
Bereich Bernkastel '84 (£–2).
Uerziger Schwarzlay Riesling '84 (£2–2.50).
Muscadet '84 (£2–2.50). Dry.
Frascati Fontana Candida (£2.50–3). Dry.

REDS

Cabernet Vino da Tavolo (£–2).
Bulgarian Cabernet Sauvignon (£–2).
House Claret (£2–2.50).

Côtes du Rhône '82 (£2.50–3).
Bulgarian Mountain Cabernet Sauvignon (£2.50–3).
Cabernet Haut Poitou (£2.50–3).
Special Reserve Pinot Noir Burgundy (£3+).

SPARKLING WINES

Blanquette de Limoux (£3+).
House Champagne (£3+).

SHERRY

Garvey San Patricio Fino (£3+).

PORT & MADEIRA

Dow LBV '79 Port (£3+).
Henriques & Henriques Madeiras (£3+).

WM LOW AND LOWFREEZE

WHITES

Lutomer Laski Riesling (£–2).
Lambrusco (£–2).
Niersteiner Berncastle (£2–2.50).
Piesporter (£2–2.50).
$1\frac{1}{2}$ litres of Soave (£3+). Dry.
Black Tower and Blue Nun (£2.50–3).

REDS

Lambrusco (£–2).
Valpolicella (in $1\frac{1}{2}$ litres) (£3+).
Le Piat d'Or (£2.50–3).

SWEET WINE

Bordeaux Blanc (£2–2.50).

SPARKLING WINES

Piemontello (just fizzy) (£–2).
Moscato Spumante (£2.50–3).
Taittinger Champagne (£3+).

SHERRY

British QC (£–2), Hudson & Cooper and Kings Head Cream
(£2–2.50).
Croft and Harvey's (£3+).

PORT

Cockburn's (£3+).

WILSONS WINES

WHITES

Romanian Riesling de Banat (£–2).
Hungarian Tramini (£–2).
Bulgarian Mehana (£–2).
Romanian Gewurtztraminer (sweetish) (£2–2.50).

REDS

Romanian Madchentraube (sweetish) (£–2).
Bulgarian Mehana (£–2).
Bulgarian Sakar Mountain (£2–2.50).
Bulgarian Mavrud (£2–2.50).
Hungarian Pinot Noir (£–2).

SWEET WINE

Romanian Pietroasele (£–2).

A FEW 'DIFFERENT' WINES

Peter Dominic – Sparkling Red Burgundy. Algerian Red Infuriator.

Davisons – Sparkling Riesling Italico Martini.

The Russian Shop – Sparkling white and red Krim. Crimean Red.

Sainsbury's – De-alcoholized Jung's and Light Masson. Quinta da Bacalhôa (Portugal).

Tanners – Sweet Loire, Moulin Touchais '55 & '69. Franken wine.

Townend – Baden wine. Sealaks New Zealand.

Wilsons Wines – Romanian Mädchentraube white and red.

Bottoms Up – Hungarian Somlo Furmint and Sopron Nagyburgundi.

Majestic Wine Warehouses – Bulgarian Sakar Mountain, Sweet Samos Muscat.

Waitrose – Romanian Riesling de Banat. Sweet Jurançon.

Dickens Wine House – Chilean wines.

Sherston Wine Company – Yugoslavian Sweet Red Muscat Hamburg.

Gough Brothers – Israeli Palwin No. 10.

Grandways — 1½ litres of Capricco (Bolzano).

Safeway – Raimat Abadia (Spain).

Threshers – White Dão (Portugal).

Unwins – Château Musar (Lebanon).

Blayney Wines – Est Est Est (Italian).

Booths – Amorone (Italian).

Oddbins – A Moroccan red wine.

Del Monico – Israeli wines.

Morris's Wine Stores – Sake (Japan).

Tesco – Falkensteiner (Austrian).

Dolamore – Algerian. Bulgarian Sakar Mountain and Mavrud.

Fullers – Grão Vasco red and white (Portugal).

Julian Flook – Tocai white Cesari (Italy).

Peatling & Cawdron – Giumarra Vineyards Colombard (U.S.A.).

Eldridge Pope – Sparkling Kir (Luxembourg).
Lay & Wheeler – Vintage Madeira.
Foodrite – Eiswein.
Whynot Wine Warehouses – Sparkling Red Burgundy.
The Victoria Wine Company – Marques de Alella, sweet and heavy white.

ABOUT THE AUTHOR

James Page-Roberts writes a weekly wine column for the *Andover Advertiser*, and contributes to *Wessex Life*, *Winemaker*, *The Edge* and *The Financial Times*.

He is the author of *Vines In Your Garden* (Argus Books), runs his own vineyard in Hampshire and is a member of the Circle of Wine Writers.

He would like to thank his wife, Barbara, for the use of her palate and knowledge, Ilze Sissons for reading the initial manuscript and John Wright, with his publishing knowledge, for its development.